THE DON'T SWEAT GUIDE
FOR GRANDPARENTS

THE DON'T SWEAT GUIDE
FOR GRANDPARENTS

Making the Most of Your Time
with Your Grandchildren

By the Editors of Don't Sweat Press
Foreword by Richard Carlson, Ph.D.,
author of the bestselling *Don't Sweat the Small Stuff*

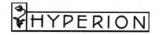

New York

ISBN 0-7868-8719-2

FIRST EDITION

10 9 8 7 6 5 4 3 2 1

Contents

Foreword

Grandparents are a gift to the world! It is from their love that we are here to begin with. I think of my own grandparents with great fondness, as my children do theirs. In fact, a huge number of people I've met and known over the years love, admire and respect their grandparents as much as anyone else in this world. I only hope my grandchildren (if I'm lucky enough to have them someday) will feel that way about me!

Grandparents are special people, often with extraordinary wisdom. They have raised children of their own, and have learned from their successes as well as their mistakes. Many have learned to be patient, reflective and extremely giving of their time, energy and love. My observation of grandparents over the years has been that they are generally calmer and less reactive than their children. When I've asked them why this is the case, many have told me, "It's because I've learned to stop sweating the small stuff."

The editors of Don't Sweat Press have written what I think of as a celebration of grandparents. The selections were created to be a source of inspiration and additional wisdom. And because, like parenting, being a grandparent (as wonderful as it is) can also be stressful at times, the strategies in this book have been created to ease some of that tension. They can have the effect of making the tasks associated with grandparenting even more joyful and fulfilling.

Recently, a grandmother joked with me, saying, "The best thing about being a grandparent is that you can enjoy your grandkids—and then give them back." A moment later she added, "I'm kidding, of course. The best thing about being a grandparent is that you get to know that you helped to create this beautiful person—your own grandchild—and that he or she is a part of your life." The love and pride she felt radiated from her, as it does from so many other grandparents.

If you are a grandparent, I'd like to thank you for the work you have done and the love you have provided. I hope you enjoy this book, and that it helps to reinforce the joy you receive from being a grandparent. It was written from a place of love—and hopefully, it will be received that way as well.

Treasure the gift of being a grandparent,
Richard Carlson
Pleasant Hill, CA, June 2001

THE DON'T SWEAT GUIDE
FOR GRANDPARENTS

1.

Understand That
You're a New Person

Becoming a grandparent transforms you in the most wonderful ways. You become a new person with a new role, identity, and relationship to others. It's an exciting time that holds the promise of rich emotional rewards with a growing family. It's also a time that can lead you to pause a moment and begin a process of self-examination.

Sometimes this self-examination produces mixed emotions, because when your children have children, you realize how far you've come in life. Facing your own aging can be difficult, and few situations bring it closer to home than being called "Grandma" or "Grandpa." The idea that becoming grandparents somehow means that you're suddenly "old" is outdated. Today, nothing could be further from the truth. There are no real, definitive boundaries that have been crossed simply because your family has grown to a third generation. Grandparenting today means being vital, up-to-date, active, and involved. You can choose to spend time thinking about your own aging, or you can use your longevity to enrich the lives of your children and your grandchildren.

When you have grandchildren, your relationship with your children changes, as well. While you will have opportunities to become closer than ever, it's also a time when they will stand on their own even more. You used to jump right in to help them when they were kids, but now you find yourself holding back lest you be seen as "butting in." Their responsibilities as parents can be challenging to them, and maybe even a little scary, so stand by. At some point (probably) they will ask for your experienced advice.

At this stage in your life, you may have grown accustomed to being alone and living on your own. Even if your children are a large presence, the introduction of small children into the family once again can be quite a change. If you're a first-timer to grandparenthood, it's normal to feel a bit apprehensive about this exciting new role. The most important thing to keep in mind is that good grandparents are made over time. Using your experience and wisdom gained throughout the years, you will grow into your role as surely as you grew into parenthood. Look back on your own experiences as a new parent and the influence your grandparents had on you. Reflecting on the past can develop the understanding and forgiving nature so important to your role as grandparents now.

Most of all, being a grandparent gives great meaning to these later years of your life. As a grandparent, you'll always have plenty to do. You are an important, necessary part of your three-generation family. There are great joys to be found in grandparenthood—get ready to embrace them all.

2.

Remember That You're
Their *Grand*parents

Following this strategy can be much easier said than done. You have years of experience as a parent, so you'll have a natural tendency to act like one, not only to your grandchildren, but to your children again. It's almost a given that parents and grandparents are likely to disagree over one or more child-rearing choices. Knowing this up front and developing ways to deal with it can cool the friction and prevent things from getting out of hand.

One of the most difficult things to remember is that, in most cases, it's not your responsibility to raise your grandchildren. Carrying around the notion that it is your job will put great stress on your relationship with your children. If you respect your children as parents and encourage them to do their own parenting, you will be fulfilling one of the greatest roles of grandparenting: being understanding and supportive of everyone in your family.

If ever there was a time to keep from giving advice unless it's asked for, it's now. Your children will learn to parent through experience and struggle, just as you did. Be there to answer questions, lend a hand, be a sounding board, or give a good, warm hug when necessary. Just as you learn and grow in your grandparenting experience, your children will grow as parents by doing, sometimes making mistakes, and doing better the next time.

One of the best ways to be supportive of your children is to tell them that you want to be consistent and follow their lead. Ask what the rules are for your grandchildren—which are rigid, and which can be bent now and then if a situation allows for it. Above all, be a good listener. Listen not only to your grandchildren, but to your children as they work their way through the ins and outs of parenthood. If they're having problems, you don't have to jump in to save the day. You may do far more for your children by not acting and listening instead. It shows your children that you believe in them and are willing to let them find their own path, but that you're standing at the ready to pitch in and help if they want you to do so.

It's a delicate balancing act to go from being a parent to being a grandparent. Remember whose parents you are, and that when they need help, your children will come to you. In fact, they will always need you, and their new role as parents will only enhance the relationship that you already share.

3.

Get Yourself in Balance

We've all been through times when life seems to career out of control. Work grows into too much work; we manage to turn social situations into social obligations; even enjoyable activities like a weekly golf game can become routine and required, taking all the fun out of it! People pull on us from all directions, and it's natural to try to please everyone all at once. There are so many roles to fill—parent, spouse, coworker or boss, teacher, sibling—and now, you're a grandparent, too.

If you have too much on your plate, it may be time to get your life in balance by making some changes in your priorities. Even little changes can allow you to get a better handle on the many things you might be juggling so that you can function with less stress and more inner calm. Most importantly, you want to make room in your life for grandparenting, because giving of your time is what's most important to your children and your grandchildren.

How can you do this? One way is to look at your obligations

and responsibilities and prioritize them. Ask yourself a few questions: Are you a workaholic? If so, can you ease up on your duties and responsibilities, perhaps by delegating to others, to allow yourself more time for your family? Do you have so many social obligations that perhaps you don't even find them enjoyable anymore? Answering yes to this question may show that you could benefit from not always saying yes to every invitation that comes your way. Once you commit to straightening out your priorities, you'll find that your life will become less hectic, and you'll be ready to take on your duties as a grandparent.

It's said that time flies when you're having fun. Well, time also seems to fly when you're not paying attention. You don't want to suddenly realize that time has passed you by, and that you've lost that time you wanted to spend with your grandchildren. Remember, the weeks are long, but the years are short. Children grow up quickly, and your window of opportunity to be an active and influential part of their lives is relatively small. Make the time now to share with your family. You'll be glad later that you made your grandchildren top priorities in your life.

4.

Develop the Family "Team"

The goal of this strategy is to cultivate a sense of cooperation and togetherness by uniting the whole family as a team—one that works together for everyone's benefit while respecting each other's unique personalities and beliefs. This can head off the "us against them" feeling that can often develop when a family grows to three generations.

Parents, caught in the middle between grandparents and grandchildren, can often feel pressured from both sides. Grandchildren may complain to grandparents about everything from strict bedtimes to the colors of their bicycles. In order to keep the peace, grandparents may act in ways that unintentionally produce the opposite effect, creating an "us against them" feeling. Giving your adult children unsolicited advice on parenting can complicate matters and further widen the gap of misunderstanding between generations, yet you can get everyone to communicate on the same level and close the gap by forming a family team.

Being the eldest of the family, think of yourself as the coach. As such, your duties include passing along your knowledge and skills to the other team members and fostering an atmosphere of cooperation and togetherness. One way to do this is to hold regular team meetings where you, as coach, act as the communications center for the family. Here, in this safe environment, everyone in the family can speak up about what's on their minds and know that other family team members will listen. Use the meeting as a place to set standards and insure that you are all on the same page regarding the grandchildren. You can work to iron out disagreements and offer solutions to problems. But most significantly, in this busy world full of distractions, it's a time when the family can be together with no other agenda than to be a family. Problems aren't the only things that might be discussed at team meetings—bring your good news, too. Everyone can share their successes and joys, as well as their thoughts and ideas for constructive change.

You, the coach, can also set examples and be a role model for the rest of the team. For example, making cooperation and stress reduction a personal goal will set the tone for the whole team. As family members see you striving to live a more peaceful life with compassion and understanding for others, they can be encouraged to follow suit. You show the rest of the team that it's possible for everyone to work together for mutual benefit.

Team meetings can also be wonderful learning experiences

when everyone is given the opportunity to be both teacher and student. As you all learn more about each other, it will become easier to relate to each person's unique experience. Don't be afraid to bring up difficult topics—if someone in the family is upset, you need to encourage honest, constructive discussion to help soothe and dissolve angry feelings.

You may need to feel your way through the process at first, and it may even be awkward simply because it's a new experience. But the benefits of such open sharing and closeness are well worth the effort to form the family team. And don't forget one of the most important functions of the grandparents as coach—to cheer everyone else on to being their very best.

5.

Start (and End) Each Visit
with a Clean Slate

Children are children—in addition to the laughter, hugs, kisses, and love that they bring, they might spill things, speak without thinking, knock things over, or get upset and cry. When they hit those little bumps in the road, remind yourself that dwelling on such incidents does nothing to get you all back on a happy track. What's done is done, so dry their tears and wipe the slate clean.

Whether your grandchildren visit you once a week or once a year, starting and ending each visit with a clean slate may be one of the most important and loving things you can do for them—and for you. Call it another simple act of forgiveness. This doesn't mean that you should accept intentionally destructive or bad behavior, however. If that occurs, you must deal with it in the best way you know how. But then you should let it go, too. Your time together will be more special and memorable if you move your focus away from any negative incidents which have already passed.

Time is always precious, so try to spend visits with your grandchildren in the most positive ways you can. Remember that the most important thing you can ever leave your grandchildren is wonderful memories of time spent with you. If you start and end each visit with a clean slate, you will all be left with warm, loving feelings to tide you over until the next visit.

6.

Make Peace with the Mess

Let's face it, kids make messes. They spill drinks, drop crumbs throughout the house, leave toys everywhere, and touch walls with dirty hands. They don't intend to make a mess, but it's just part of being a kid. Their job is to get into everything and explore. The interesting part about kids' messes is that they seem to defy most laws of physics: The smaller the child, the bigger the mess.

Grandparents sometimes have trouble with the messes children make. Once your own children left home, you probably grew accustomed to a more tidy household. So when your grandchildren come to visit, and sometimes when you visit them in their home, their messy ways can get on your nerves. You might think that the best way to head off mass disorganization is to try to tidy up as the mess occurs, attempting to nip it in the bud. But this can get quite stressful for everyone involved if you're constantly fretting about things dropped here and there, a coat draped over a chair, a dirty glass left on the kitchen counter. The untidiness becomes your only focus, when in reality, the mess is probably only a tiny part of time spent with your grandkids.

The best thing you can do is to simply make peace with the mess and accept it as part of having children in the house again. You can tidy up later and do so without anxiety if you learn to stay calm and accept the situation at hand. This will keep frustrations at bay and allow you to enjoy your grandchildren much more.

Leave the mess until later, provided there are no safety hazards involved and nothing about the mess will cause any damage to furniture, carpeting, or clothing. If toys are spread all over the living room, you might clear a small path for passing through and leave the rest until the little ones take their nap.

You can also make peace with the mess if you help create it! The added advantage to this idea is that you can guide the direction the mess is going. Suppose you see your young grandchildren outside playing in a mud puddle. Why not get on some old clothes, go outside, and join them? It's probably been a long time since you made mud pies yourself, but offering to teach them how to do that will certainly allow you to relate to them on a fun level. It also allows you control the mess by keeping it outside, and then making sure that everyone gets cleaned up carefully without making a further mess in the house. Best of all, you've spent some quality play time with your grandchildren, and you'll probably have to admit later that you had a ball playing in the mud.

Allowing children's messes to upset and frustrate you takes

away from the wonderful experience of grandparenting. Accepting what is and learning to work with it and around it will help you keep peace within the family and make visits more enjoyable for everyone. Messes aren't the end of the world, and if the rug does get a stain, so what? In the bigger picture, a piece of carpet can be replaced. But when children grow up so quickly that you could blink and miss a few years, time spent together is irreplaceable.

7.

Remember the Things
You Weren't Allowed to Do

You might remember certain things you weren't "allowed" to do as a child. You weren't supposed to get dirty, make noise, get wet in the rain, or eat dessert before dinner. You could never understand why adults got so upset if you did these things, because sometimes doing them simply couldn't have mattered at the time. Today, more than ever, children are "not allowed" to do many things that in reality are harmless. The reasons that parents will not allow kids to do them aren't always good or rational.

Children often become upset when they are told they can't do something. They can become even more frustrated when you can't explain to them in simple terms *why* they can't do it. Remembering what you weren't allowed to do as a child may help you stop automatically stifling your grandkids and let them have some adventures in life. Accepting these little adventures and learning to keep from being overly protective can reduce your level of stress and make grandparenting an experience beyond the ordinary.

An "adventure" doesn't have to mean going over a waterfall in a barrel. Most kids hear the same simple, common admonition over and over: "Don't run!" The fact is that kids *should* run and play—skinned knees happen, and it's okay, it's part of life. Of course, you'll want to make sure they're not running around in the street or in the house, where they might knock things over. But running and playing outdoors in a safe environment such as a playground is healthy—a lot healthier than sitting in front of the TV or computer for hours on end. So sit outside and watch them run and play. If you're so inclined, get up and join them in a game of tag. The trick is to remember that a lot of kids all over the world run and fall every day of the week, and it's okay for your grandchildren to do it, too.

"Don't get dirty!" is another sentence that comes out of adult mouths with such routine that it can hold little meaning for kids. Kids do get dirty. All it takes is acceptance of that fact—and some soap and water to clean them up—to avoid being bothered by something you can't control anyway.

In general, lighten up. Taking things too seriously is often the mindset responsible for dismissing things out of hand. If taking things less seriously where your grandchildren are concerned is difficult for you, try to start with something small. Be the one to teach your grandson how to ride a two-wheel bicycle. Put the training wheels on, and walk along right beside him as he rides, but do let go of the bike sometime. You'll know when he can go on his own. Soon you'll be able to let your grandchildren run and get dirty and experience all kinds of things in life that perhaps you weren't allowed to do as a child. Just remember that a lot of things kids want to do are harmless, so let them have fun.

8.

You Don't Always
Have to Do Disney World

S ometimes grandparents can get carried away trying to entertain their grandchildren. There's nothing wrong with taking them on expensive trips to grand theme parks for vacations. It's wrong, however, to think that you *have* to do this—or any similar big productions—consistently in order to be loved by them.

Think back to your fondest memories of your own grandparents. You'll probably remember the simple, everyday types of things you shared: reading the Sunday comics; going for ice cream cones on a bright sunny afternoon; building a snowman together in the backyard; baking cookies; playing board games on the back porch on balmy nights. In all of these cases, it wasn't the activity that was memorable. It was doing the activity with your grandparents, and loving every minute of it, that sticks with you.

Make it a priority to introduce your grandchildren to the simple things in life. Doing this moderates expectations and instills an appreciation for everyday things. Take them on walks in the fall to collect colored leaves, or spend time on a lake shore breathing the fresh air and skipping stones across the water's surface. Your grandchildren are growing up in a busier and more complex world than you did. Simple times encourage something much more important and lasting: bonding and togetherness. This will be your greatest gift to them.

This isn't to say that big productions are always bad. In fact, big adventures are best when they occur infrequently so that children can learn to appreciate them and your generosity in giving them. Additionally, we can have a tendency to always want to "one-up" ourselves for the kids. Disney World is a tough act to follow, so being in the mode of topping yourself each time will find its limitations pretty quickly.

The fact is that you can make many of the simple things into special events. Baking cookies together, for example, can turn into quite the culinary lesson if you make flavored icings, add decorations, and create one-of-a-kind shapes. Making a collage can go beyond cutting images from old magazines and newspapers if you include family photos: Finding these old photos can involve members of the family from all over the world, creating an ongoing project just for you and your grandkids.

So let go of the idea that you have to make a big production of entertaining your grandchildren. The simple things done together will go down in family history and show them that in doing *anything* together, the operative word is "together."

9.

Remember the Three Things That Grandchildren Want and Need: Attention, Attention, and Attention

Remember how excited you were when you got to visit with your grandparents? From the first moment you saw them, you wanted to soak up as much of their attention as you possibly could. With grandparents, that's usually easy to do. It didn't matter to you whether your grandfather was a policeman or a farmer, a scientist or a steelworker. You didn't care one bit if grandma was a doctor or a teacher, a nurse or a homemaker. What mattered was that your grandparents did a lot of things to make you feel special, and they gave you plenty of love. They may have greeted you with a gift of some sort, but more than anything, it was their time and attention that made you feel like you were the most important person in the world.

It's no different for your grandchildren. When they visit with you, they want and need very little except your love and attention.

They want to hear you read their favorite stories to them at bedtime; to help you bake cookies; to learn how to fish from you, the expert. They want to read Sunday comics with you, see you in the bleachers at their softball games, or go to fun new movies with you. The time you spend together doing things, and your hugs and smiles, will be remembered much longer than any material gifts.

It's okay to give gifts to your grandchildren, of course, and surprising them with presents can be a big part of the fun of grandparenting. But too often, it's easy for grandparents to fall into the habit of giving material gifts, and grandchildren then learn to expect them. The problem is that the grandchildren want more, and grandparents then get caught up in trying to give bigger and better. Rather than spend time worrying about what presents to give, you should simply spend time with them. Giving them the gifts of your love, time, and attention will help them learn to appreciate what they already have and help them feel the love in your heart.

10.

Learn the Fine Art
of Saying No

A notion exists that grandparents will always say yes to just about everything their grandchildren ask for. In many ways, grandparents themselves go along with that notion. After all, they may say to themselves (or their exasperated children), what are grandparents for?

It's a mistake to want your grandchildren to see you as an endless source of whatever they want. For many reasons—some of which you can explain to them and some of which you can't—you just may have to say no. Unfortunately, saying no can cause grandchildren to whine, complain, cry, and even throw tantrums, which is often why grandparents *don't* say no as much as they probably should. The key is to learn the fine art of saying no and not feel guilty about it, while you strive to create a win-win situation at the same time.

Learning to say no will serve you well in your dealings with grandchildren. The key is that before you say no, you must be patient and do a little detective work to find out *why* your grandchildren want what they're asking for. Suppose your granddaughter wants a fast-food meal-in-a-box, but you'd rather eat somewhere else a bit more to your taste. Just saying no will probably upset her, so ask her straight out why she wants that particular fast-food meal. You may discover that she actually wants the little toy that comes with it. You really don't mind her having the toy, so you can offer her an alternative: You'll take her to a discount store to get a small toy, but then you get to choose where you'll eat. The child learns compromise, and you and she get to spend a lot of one-on-one time together, going shopping and having lunch.

You may not always have an alternative to offer, however. In this case, saying no without feeling guilty will take practice on your part. Accepting that they can't have everything all the time can help your grandchildren focus more on what they do have and learn to enjoy it now, in the present moment—and that's the real lesson.

11.

Refine the Art
of Saying Yes

The fine art of saying no notwithstanding, grandparents are still going to frequently say yes to their grandchildren. There's nothing wrong with that most of the time, and after all, grandparents will be grandparents. But saying yes indiscriminately and too often, particularly against parents' wishes, is a common cause of stress and disagreements in families. Grandparents can refine the art of saying yes to make compromise and harmony the goals in the end.

One cause of great conflict is when grandparents say yes to a request that the child's parents have already denied. This pits the parents against the grandparents and can unwittingly teach children that if Mom and Dad say no, go to Grandma and Grandpa for the desired result. This is probably not the message you want to send your grandchildren, nor do you want them to always think of you in that manner. It's possible to inadvertently go against your children's wishes, so if grandchildren come to you with requests, it's a good idea to determine if they've already asked their parents. This way, you can support your children's decision while explaining to your grandchildren that they just can't always have whatever they want, even from those who love them the most.

The perfect time for you to play the grandparental role of mediator is anytime your children have denied a grandchild's request and the child then comes to you in hopes of still getting what he wants. You may be able to explain to your grandson why his parents said no. Or just offer support for his feelings without passing judgement on the parents' decision. Perhaps because you are not as close to the situation, you can offer a compromise that his parents have not thought about. As the third party, you can be a calming influence on both your children and grandchildren. This is well worth your efforts, as it can only lead to more peace and less conflict in the family.

12.

Accept That
No Two Are Alike

Grandchildren are like snowflakes—no two of them are exactly alike. Each child has different likes, dislikes, interests, desires, strengths, and weaknesses, and a unique personality. Children may also have completely different needs from one another. As grandparents, it's important to accept this fact.

It takes time and effort to discover children's individuality in order to relate to them more fully and provide for their separate needs. Some children are outgoing and make friends easily; others may be more shy and withdrawn, perhaps needing a little help from parents and grandparents to bloom socially. Some kids are more introspective than others and like—and need—a healthy dose of solitude. Learning to recognize differences like these in your grandchildren will help you to develop closer, happier relationships with them.

Acceptance also includes managing your expectations. Just

because one grandchild is a good athlete doesn't mean you should expect a sibling to be equally as proficient. That child may, in fact, not even like sports and rather read books, play a musical instrument, or learn to ride a horse. You should not only allow, but also encourage, such individuality when it shows itself. Leading children away from natural tendencies toward something more suitable to others is a recipe for conflict. Encouraging your grandchildren to be themselves shows that you accept them as they are, and your acceptance is one of the things that they want most from you.

Appreciating grandchildren who are the same in some ways, yet very different in others, can be a beautiful experience. It reminds us that we do not live in a "cookie-cutter" world, and that we are surrounded by individuals from whom we can learn new ideas and different ways of thinking. And besides, if your grandchildren's interests run the gamut from sports to music to science, look at how much you'll have to talk about to your friends!

13.

Every Child Is an Artist

Pablo Picasso said, "Every child is an artist. The problem is how to remain an artist once he grows up." Along the way to adulthood, children meet critics, teachers, and others who might crush their creativity and sense of exploration, usually without meaning to do so. Unfortunately, the result can be that children may stop sharing their inner voices and expressing what's in their hearts.

Resist the urge to "correct" your grandchild's artistic efforts. "Don't color that horse orange!" is something a well-meaning parent, grandparent, or teacher might say to a child expressing creativity. But the truth is that kids *can* color horses orange—why not? It certainly won't hurt anything. You might consider that an interesting, fresh perspective in a curious young mind led to the unusual choice of color. It would be a shame to dampen the creative curiosity that can drive a child to seek more knowledge.

It may be difficult to curb your desire to "correct" your grandchildren when they color horses orange or draw three arms on stick figures. But giving children free rein to imagine and express themselves can truly boost your spirits. In fact, you might sit right down beside them and join in. Pick up a paint brush, or dip your hands into the fingerpaints, and let your own imagination fly. You may gain some interesting insights into your grandchildren—and yourself.

If your grandchildren continue to show artistic leanings, you might take them to a local museum, or sign them up for art classes. Your encouragement of their desires to express themselves will warm their spirits and strengthen the bonds between you.

14.

Let Them Talk

People need to be heard almost as much as they need food, water, and shelter. Children are no different. When kids get excited and get into "chatterbox" mode, it's easy for adults to feel overwhelmed and be tempted to tune them out. It may be where the old expression comes from: "Children should be seen and not heard."

Throw that old expression out the window! Children need to be heard as much as anyone else. Running a busy household, work, or social obligations can often distract parents. Your grandchildren may seek out sympathetic grandparents to listen to them. If you let them talk and really listen to what they're saying, you show your grandchildren that they—and what they have to say—are important to you. Just like adults, children need to feel respected and understood. Listening to what kids have to say gives them that respect and understanding.

By being a good listener, you're a good role model for teaching your grandchildren how to do the same. Experts say that children's listening patterns are established by the time they are five years old.

If you are patient and listen to children's thoughts without cutting them off or finishing their sentences, they will learn that this is how people communicate and build close bonds.

It's important to listen for the feelings in your grandchildren's words. Sometimes we hear only words, but not the message that's coming from within. This is especially true of children, who may couch fears and doubts in seemingly innocuous questions. Your granddaughter might say to you, "Are my friends going to go to preschool, too?" If you answer, "Yes, Allison and Teresa are going to the same school," you've answered her question but maybe not addressed the message. You might say, "Yes, they are. How do you feel about going to school—are you a little nervous about it?" Being fearful of going to school may be what the child is really trying to communicate.

The key to truly listening to grandchildren and hearing those messages is to open your heart along with your ears. It shows them that their feelings are as important as their words. You can let your grandchildren know that you're willing and able to listen by inviting them to talk. If something seems to be troubling a child, ask, "Do you want to tell me about it?" If there's nothing wrong and you just want to talk, say, "I'd like to hear how your day was—tell me about what you did." Then open up, listen, soak it all in.

As a grandparent, being a good listener to your grandchildren *and* your children is a wonderful gift that shows your love, support, and understanding. You may be surprised at what you can learn when you open up to hear what others have to say.

15.

Introduce Them to Gratitude

Expressing gratitude is easy, though we never seem to do it enough. There are so many things to be grateful for in life: our friends and family, our homes, careers, nature, and the world around us. If you take time every day to think about the many people and things you have to be thankful for, it's difficult for negativity to creep into your thoughts. This is a wonderful concept to pass along to your grandchildren, and there's no time like the present to get started.

Two little words, "thank you," are a good start, so use them freely in front of your grandchildren. Say these words to someone who gives you a gift, or does a special favor for you—or simply say thank you to someone for being your friend and being in your life. In fact, say thank you to your grandchildren—just for being your grandchildren. Then thank your children, as well. Oddly, the people who mean the most to us are often the ones we thank the least.

Being kind and doing kind deeds is another way to show

someone, through actions, that you are grateful for their presence. Enlist your grandchildren to help you with random acts of kindness, little gifts from the heart to friends, family, or even strangers. Helping an elderly person with her groceries or leaving some cash or canned goods at a local soup kitchen qualifies. The simple act of being kind shows a deep gratitude for life. Instilling this idea in your grandchildren is one of the greatest gifts you can give them.

Best of all, you get to bask in the glow of the wonderful feelings that come from sharing this philosophy with your grandchildren, especially when you hear them say thank you to people close to them. Then you know that you've had an impact in their lives.

16.

You're Not a Mind-Reader, So Ask Questions

One of the best ways for grandparents to avoid conflict and misunderstandings in the family is to learn their children's ideas and philosophies on child rearing. This way, you won't accidentally go against their rules or inadvertently undermine their authority when you are with your grandchildren. You may think that you already know what they believe regarding raising children. It's easy to assume that they will basically follow the same philosophies that you did in raising them. While they may indeed use you as role models, they won't necessarily do everything the same way you did.

This doesn't mean that your children's new ideas are wrong—they're just different from yours. You may not want to ask questions so you don't seem to be "out of it" where new child-rearing theories are concerned. But there is no such thing as a foolish question, so don't be afraid to ask your children for specifics about rules, foods, entertainment, bedtimes, discipline, and more, to avoid clashes that will have your grandchildren in the middle. In fact, this is a perfect topic to bring up during family team meetings, which are designed to be a forum for open and honest discussion. Make it clear that you're asking questions with everyone's best interests in mind, and to strive for consistency between your home and theirs.

This is also a good time for you to offer support to your children by asking them what they need and want from you. Is there something you've done that they would prefer you don't do in the future? Is there anything you don't do that they would appreciate your doing? Questions such as these let your children know that you truly want to work as a team and that you're willing to make changes in your behavior if that's what's best.

Finally, accept the answers you receive, even if you don't completely agree with them. At the heart of this strategy is the desire to be loving and supportive of your children and to provide a peaceful family environment for everyone. By asking questions to learn more about your children's beliefs, and then respecting those beliefs, you show them your love and commitment to them and to your grandchildren.

17.

Expand Your Expectations

Grandparents want their grandchildren to achieve the loftiest of goals and be happy in life. It's natural to want the very best for those you love, and you may have certain ideas about what directions your grandchildren should take in order to live happy, successful lives. But realize that their natural talents and tendencies may point them in different directions. Your grandchildren, as individuals, may choose paths other than what you have in mind.

This doesn't mean that they won't live rich, full, and happy lives, of course. But it does mean that they will—and should—march to the beat of their own drum. Unfortunately, we often expect our loved ones to do certain things and behave in certain ways, which can lead to frustration, disappointment, and unhappiness. It can be difficult to let go of these expectations, so a better strategy might be to try to expand them. It sounds funny at first, but expanding your expectations doesn't mean that you make them bigger. Rather, you expand the range of your expectations to encompass your grandchildren's individuality and personalities. In other words, if you can't make your expectations go away entirely, at least make them realistic.

A grandson who hates math isn't likely to lean toward science as a vocation, so having expectations for his engineering career isn't realistic. Neither is hoping for a dancer's career for a young woman who might not be as graceful as the ballet requires. Nowhere can expectations be stronger than in the case of family-run businesses, where it's often expected that a grandchild will follow in the parent's and grandparent's footsteps. Sometimes our expectations are fairly simple—we would like children to take an interest in a particular topic which holds no interest for them at all. Generally, no amount of pushing or coaxing will change that.

Any time you demand that others meet your expectations, you set them and yourself up for disappointments. By expanding your expectations to become more realistic, you create an atmosphere of encouragement and positive reinforcement. When your grandchildren know that they can come to you to openly discuss their talents, interests, and options in life without fear of becoming victims of unrealistic expectations, you will truly fulfill one of the most important roles of grandparenting.

18.

Believe (and Make Believe) Again

Do you ever sit quietly and watch your grandchildren play, perhaps without their knowing it? Do you find a smile spreading across your face when you do? Maybe that smile comes from being reminded of how simple life was when you were a child, when you had nothing to worry about. You could make up the kind of world you wanted to be in and pretend you could be anything in the world. Believe it or not, you can get that feeling back again, even for a while, by joining your grandchildren at play.

Playing make-believe with your grandchildren can be a terrific bonding experience that just might bring some lightheartedness into your life. It doesn't matter if it's been a long time since you last let go and lightened up in this way. Playing together from time to time can help make problems seem far less serious whenever they do come up.

We all know that adults can be far too serious about life. We tend to expect things to be a certain way, and if they don't turn out to be exactly that way, we can become frustrated. Those who are too serious can make a mountain out of a spilled glass of milk or a big emergency out of a little tussle between young grandchildren. Life can be difficult for others forced to be around such constant seriousness.

So lighten up—go ahead and join the kids! Pretend you're John Wayne on a cattle drive with the other little cowboys. Or be the patient who is cared for by the cute little nurse and doctor. When you can become part of your grandchildren's make-believe, they will definitely see you in a different light, and most likely, they will want to see you more and more. It's just so much fun to be around someone who is willing and able to play from time to time. There's a Latin proverb that says, "Believe that you have it, and you have it." Believe that you can make believe again—and you can.

19.

Remember That
It Matters Not

Do you ever sit and daydream about your grandchildren's future? It's a perfectly honorable pastime, and certainly a creative one. You might see yourself surrounded by family, watching your grandson at the altar on his wedding day. Or perhaps you're standing proudly in the crowd at a college graduation, clapping and cheering when your granddaughter walks up on stage to collect her well-earned degree. Maybe you see them even farther in the future, happily playing with children of their own.

What you surely *won't* recall years from now, when you're actually witnessing great life events such as these, is the time your grandson spilled a chocolate milkshake on your new car's front seat, or when your young granddaughter dropped one of your mother's china plates, shattering it to bits. Nor will you recall the little squabbles that occurred from time to time in the family. The reason you won't remember those irritating moments is that in the greater scheme of things, they were unimportant. At the time they occurred, you may have become frustrated or angry. You may have overreacted in a way that you regretted later.

If so, you may want to daydream a little bit more about the future. It is a good exercise to play in your mind some of the greatest moments that will take place in your grandchildren's lives. It can make you realize that the little irritations you're all experiencing as they grow up simply won't matter then. So ask yourself: How much can they possibly matter now?

The car's upholstery can be cleaned. Maybe the china plate can be replaced—and maybe it can't. But it's up to you how you choose to remember the years with your grandchildren. At those times when you become annoyed or angry at life's little mishaps, you can choose to turn such small stuff into big stuff, or you can keep in mind that it doesn't matter. You'll be less likely to stay annoyed or angry for very long, and in the process become a more forgiving and accepting person.

20.

Watch What
a Smile Can Do

More than anything, a smile can dramatically change a person's appearance. A hard face becomes softer and gentler. Eyes that seem distant become sharp and bright, and you'll probably see a twinkle that wasn't there before. Even a person's mannerisms change, from slow and dull to energetic and uplifting. The best thing about a smile is that these wonderful things happen to the person who's wearing the smile *and* to the person who's on the receiving end of it!

A smile can chase the blues away, dry tears, and make the sun shine again, whether you're wearing it yourself or flashing it to others. Learning to smile in the face of the little things that can make you sweat about family life—the irritations, the quirks, the squabbles, the messes, and the things over which you have no control—can bring a lot of peace when it's needed the most. Best of all, your smile can spread to everyone else, including your grandchildren.

Sometimes in certain situations, words may be hard to say or difficult to find. Maybe a little smile can change everything in those cases. It might make only a small difference, but that's better than nothing. It's not always easy to wear a smile on your face, but it's definitely something worth practicing. When you watch what a smile can do for yourself and those around you, you'll wonder why you didn't get into the habit a long time ago.

21.

Take a Nap
When They Do

This little strategy is a wonderful way for grandparents and grandchildren to share in relaxation and stillness. You might be planning to take a nap anyway, right? Why not do it when your grandchildren do? You can give yourself a break, but still spend quality time with the kids.

You might choose a special place to take naps together. Young children can nap almost anywhere. Most kids do just fine on a floor mat like those used for naps at preschools. You might get similar mats so that you can put them in whatever room is most comfortable for you. The living room has always been a favorite napping spot, so spread out the mats and lie down together. As you all become still and your minds become quiet, you might notice something else happening. Little hearts may open up and be encouraged to talk about things that they have on their minds. Or you may suddenly have a wonderful memory from the past and decide to share it with your grandchildren in this calm, quiet environment. It's a great time for closeness, and you may even develop a ritual where you tell "nap stories" in much the same way you tell bedtime stories.

Of course, you'll eventually fall asleep. When you awaken, you'll all feel refreshed and relaxed. Any tensions that may have built up during the day may be completely gone, allowing you and your grandchildren to fully enjoy the rest of the day and each other's company.

22.

Watch a Sunset Together

S unsets are remarkable things. They inspire a sense of wonder and amazement, as well as the feeling that you're connected to nature and the world. They can calm and soothe the mind, and provide a feeling of well-being. Sunsets also have a wonderful way of bringing you into the present moment. No matter what has happened earlier that day, a brilliant sunset can make you forget everything else except its brilliance in that very moment.

Sunsets seem to be made for sharing. Taking time to watch a colorful sunset can give you and your family a period of stillness in your day; a chance to break a chain of tension and busy actions. Use this time to clear your mind, and be open to new thoughts and ideas. Replace your frazzled feelings with serenity and inspiration. Listen to your grandchildren's thoughts and observations. Wonderful discussions and caring, warm feelings will form in the waning light of a sunset.

Being able to watch a sunset with your family is something to be grateful for. Such beauty can serve as a reminder to everyone that life is an incredible gift and we shouldn't take it for granted.

23.

Surprise Them with Cards or Letters, Even if They Live in the Same Town

Children love going to the mailbox and pulling out something that has arrived just for them. It makes them feel truly special because someone took the time to sit down and write to them. Of course, you'll remember to send cards on special occasions like birthdays and holidays. But brightening your grandchildren's day with cards or letters for no special reason other than to say "I love you" truly speaks from the heart.

Even if you all live in the same town, surprise cards or letters to grandchildren can remind them that they are always in your thoughts. Phone calls are okay, but a carefully chosen card or a letter with a warm, personal message can be saved and reread for many years to come. It can be treasured in private or shared with others, because it says to the children that their grandparents love and appreciate them a great deal.

You may be tempted to mail something on a regular basis, but stop and think about the meaning of a personal, heartfelt communication. Spontaneity and surprise are the key factors to this exercise. If a letter or card arrived each week on the same day, it might not seem much different from getting a weekly subscription magazine. It becomes predictable and routine, and may lose meaning. Instead, write when you really have something to say, and this will come across to the child.

What can you write? Don't worry about quantity, which will come with practice. It's the quality of the message that's important anyway. Tell your grandchildren how much you miss them and express your feelings about them. Ask about their lives and activities, and encourage them to write you in return. Don't forget to keep their letters so that you can refer to them when you write again—this way, they know you care about their messages and are paying attention to their letters.

You might use letter-writing to pass along stories about yourself, the family, and family history. Share your own thoughts about life, and write about things that are important to them, such as school and friends. Giving letters to your grandchildren may also inspire them to become letter-writers. In this fast-paced world of cell phones and e-mail, letter-writing can be a rare and wonderful thing.

24.

Introduce Them to
Your Friends

It can be quite amusing to listen to a small child's comments on being "old," or at least what they think of as old. At age seven, being in your 70s can be nearly incomprehensible. Some children may even express fears of growing older. But you and your friends can have an opportunity to positively mold your grandchildren's views of older people and aging. Introducing your friends to your grandchildren can give kids broader exposure to people of all ages and backgrounds. As a bonus, you may even brighten the day for friends who may not have family near them.

Children who have spent quality time around elders develop an understanding, tolerance, and appreciation for them. This can help lessen "generation-gap" friction and keep peace in the family. Some discretion on your part is required, however. For example, if you have a friend who tends to be grouchy around children or doesn't particularly care for them, you should avoid making that introduction. Consider those friends who have a positive attitude and approach to life, who take things in stride and with good humor. Those are the friends who can help you show grandchildren that older people can be fun—and fun to be with.

When children enjoy experiences with elderly people, they look positively at the prospect of growing older themselves. When they spend time with you and your friends being active, enjoying life, and learning from you, it helps them see positive things in their own futures. The best part is that everyone makes new friends all around, and you get to show your grandchildren—and your friends—how important they all are in your life.

25.

Don't Complain or
List Your Troubles

For some reason, we love to talk about our problems. We talk about how busy we are, how much our backs hurt, or how expensive the insurance (or the mortgage, or the car payment, or the electric bill) has become. We can be especially good at listing our physical ills for others, perhaps out of a quest for sympathy, or just to get things off our chests. In any case, complaining or listing your troubles to your grandchildren won't gain you any grandparenting points, and if you do it habitually, it may serve to come between you and your family.

Your grandchildren simply want to be with you. But if you're having a bad day, whether for health or other reasons, sharing your mood with them can ruin your time together. It's not that they won't understand if you're having a health problem that prevents you from participating in certain activities with them. If that's the case, tell them honestly, as a matter of fact, without complaining.

Kids don't want to hear adults complain, but they will understand if you tell them the truth. Then together, you can come up with alternative plans that you can keep up with.

If your problems are any other kind of adult troubles that have no bearing on the kids, spare them the details. Troubles come and go—if you concentrate on them, they will stubbornly stick around and maybe even grow larger than they really are, leaving little room for the things in life you want to enjoy. Accepting them as part of life and letting go of the stranglehold they can have on your thoughts will set you free and make you the kind of person your family wants to be with. The trick is to be grateful for your good times, and be graceful when you're having bad ones. Let the joy you get from your grandchildren distract you and pull you through until things improve.

26.

Give Them Your
"Seal of Approval"

Children are usually told about what they're doing wrong far more often than what they're doing right. The truth is that in many cases, there may not really be a right or wrong. Adults can be so tempted to constantly correct children that they forget one simple thing: Children, like everyone else, are seeking approval for things that they do and for who they are. The next time that you find yourself ready to criticize your grandson, why not try offering him your official grandparent's seal of approval instead? Let him know how special he is to you and how much you love him just the way he is—no right or wrong involved. You'll brighten the child's day, and make him feel more secure about himself.

Criticism can sting a child, and needless criticism is especially painful. You may want to take some time to observe why you might criticize something your grandchild does for which there is no real right or wrong. Maybe it's because you're afraid of what others might think. If so, ask yourself what's really important—the opinions strangers might or might not have or your grandchild's feelings? The answer should be pretty clear. Your family's feelings should be a top priority—certainly above the thoughts and ideas of strangers. So reassure your grandson instead of criticizing him needlessly. You'll feel pretty good yourself if you give him your seal of approval, saying "I love you just the way you are," and that's something truly positive he can carry into adulthood.

27.

Show—Don't Just Tell— Your Grandchildren That You Love Them

This strategy is especially important for grandparents who don't see their grandchildren in person very often. If you live some distance apart, words can be all you have to communicate with until you can visit each other. Naturally, telling your grandchildren that you love them is extremely important. But make sure that you show your love through actions, as well, which reinforce your words and validate them.

Sometimes we say one thing and do another. We can tell our grandchildren how much they mean to us, yet when we are with them, we might not give them the time and attention they seek. This makes them wonder if what we say is really true! For this reason, what we do can be far more important in the end. So spend a lot of time with your grandchildren—you know they want your attention, and taking time to be with them reinforces your words of love and assures them that you're there for them. Hugs are another wonderful way to show your love. The physical closeness of a warm embrace will warm their hearts for a long time to come. So many people lack intimacy with their families, and few gestures can say as much as a loving hug.

Many little things in everyday life provide opportunities to show your love. Make sure you are on time for dinner with the family. Learn how to really listen to your children and grandchildren by paying attention to what they have to say. The fact is that showing your family you love them is essentially a way of life. It means being aware of the fact that sometimes your actions don't match your words, and taking steps to change that. The result—better, more loving family relationships—is well worth the effort and self-reflection.

28.

Remember What
It's Like to Be Small

Can you remember what it was like to be small, looking up at the world towering above you, surrounded by adults' knees? Even young children can get a feeling of being insignificant—think how often you hear kids say, "I can't wait to grow up!" The world can be a scary place to those who are small. When they ask for guidance or attention, try to remember what it felt like to be that small.

It can be easy for adults to brush off children's concerns. If your grandchild is worried about something that you think is silly, remember that what is silly to you can be like a monster under the bed to a child. In fact, let's suppose it's the mythical monster under the bed that your granddaughter is upset about. Rather than brush it off, or telling her, "There's no such thing, just go to bed," take a moment to put yourself in her shoes. Think back, and you'll probably remember that when you were small, most everything in the world was a big mystery—sometimes wonderful and sometimes scary. You had questions about everything. Some of the answers adults gave you satisfied you, but there was always another question sitting on the tip of your tongue, just waiting to jump out and be asked. When adults took you and your concerns seriously, you felt really good! It made you feel loved that they took the time to really listen and understand you. But if they ignored you or made fun of your curiosity, it surely made you feel embarrassed and insecure.

There is nothing more important than your loved ones' feelings. When grandchildren have concerns, or they are feeling neglected or small, remember that they *are* small compared to you, and that the world is unfamiliar to them. It's time to put aside whatever you're doing and give them your attention. You'll really connect with your grandchildren, and they're sure to remember that when they're no longer small.

29.

Teach Your Grandchildren About
Someone Special Every Day

When you were a child, was there a special person you wanted to be just like when you grew up? Maybe it was a parent, grandparent, favorite aunt or uncle, or even a neighbor. There may have been several adults you admired, including some you didn't know personally, but had learned about in school, from books, or on TV. All of these people had certain traits that made them special to you, and that's why you wanted to be like them. Your grandchildren think you're special, of course, and you can give them a lot of positive role models to admire by teaching them about other special people and their accomplishments.

It shouldn't be difficult to think of a special person to talk about every day of the week if you wanted to do so. Introduce your grandchildren to these special people, either in person or through books, films, or stories. Talk about what makes them special and what traits these people have that your grandchildren might want to acquire. When you show your grandchildren how special people can be, you can inspire them to find ways to be special themselves. Talking about others who have made a difference reminds you, too, about loving, positive people. It might make you stop for a moment and check your own behavior to see what kind of example you're setting. Make sure that you can feel good about yourself and the messages you're sending. If not, it's a hint to consider some changes that can make your life more peaceful and make you a better example to others.

30.

Don't Take
Their Words Personally

Kids say what's on their minds at the moment—and it's just that: the moment. They can be unaware of the impact of their words when they're emotional, and might not understand that those words could hurt others. If they're being disciplined, their point of view makes the situation even more dramatic than it actually is. It's times like these when they might say hurtful things that they wouldn't normally say and truly don't mean. It's important for you to take these little outbursts in stride, recognize them for what they are, and move past them.

In fact, it probably won't be long until the grandchild who spoke forgets about the incident himself. If the words are particularly harsh, however, you should call his attention to what was said and explain that such outbursts can hurt people's feelings. You might say to your grandson, "I know that you're upset and you didn't mean what you said, but when you say things like that you can hurt people's feelings and make them feel very sad."

Bear in mind that there may be an element of familiarity at work here, as well. We tend to treat our family members differently from the way we treat strangers. We feel free to reveal our true selves to our families, especially when we are angry or upset. Unconsciously, we know that we are safe with our families—that we will always be loved despite our negative words. While you may accept that as a fact of family life, you can also start now to teach your grandchildren respect for family members' feelings. But when they do get angry and say things they don't mean, remember to not take it personally and know that they really do love you.

31.

Remember That
You're Being Watched

Kids are great imitators. They love to watch adults and learn from them, even mimicking what they do or pretending to be them. Children can be particularly inclined to watch and learn from their grandparents, whom they love and look up to as role models. Realizing this, you should make an effort to pay more attention to your behavior the next time you find yourself getting a bit hot under the collar about something. It could be that you're being watched.

This doesn't mean that you're being spied on, but then again, with grandchildren, you just never know. Even when you're alone or think you're alone, there might be little eyes peeking at you from somewhere. So if you're acting uptight or short-tempered about something that's really not worth getting upset about, think about the possibility that your grandchildren are watching you. You surely don't want them to see you behaving that way. And if you have a habit of overreacting to certain situations, your grandchildren could very well learn to overreact to these things, as well. If you remember that their curious eyes are watching, this can act like a reset button for you.

We normally don't want to base our behavior or actions on what others might think, but it's different in the case of impressionable young grandchildren. Whether they're watching you or not, the real lesson from this strategy is to recognize when life's irritations are getting to you, and get your perspective back. You could be setting an example that will make an impression on your grandchildren's minds, so make sure the example is one you want to set.

32.

Fire Them Up!

Firing up the grandchildren doesn't mean that grandparents should get them all *worked* up and unruly. This is about firing up their sense of wonder and thirst for knowledge, things that will serve them well for a lifetime. Knowledge is what opens minds and leads to understanding and acceptance.

Kids look to grandparents to teach them about the world around them, as well as to provide wisdom and advice. They may be more open to visiting museums, libraries, or art galleries with grandparents than with anyone else. Take them to such places whenever you have the chance. Or try renting movies with historical content and make it an entertainment experience. Whatever you can do to fire up their desire to know more is worth the effort. They will be more confident in their own knowledge and abilities and do much better in school. But even more importantly, children who know and understand something about history, science, and culture are more able to accept the world around them as it is. Those who can live with acceptance are far more peaceful inside.

It's well within the grandparents' role to stroke a child's imagination. There's not a thing wrong with daydreaming—how else can you open your mind to new thoughts and ideas? Too many children are admonished for daydreaming, or to be more specific, for exercising their imaginations. "Stop daydreaming and do something useful!" is a common warning to kids, yet playing with the imagination can be something much more than useful. Think about Isaac Newton and Thomas Edison, and consider how useful their daydreams were to them! If your young grandson or granddaughter expresses a desire to become an astronaut, encourage that dream. Remember that kids are living in a time when the possibility is very high for that dream to become a reality. Let them know that such opportunities are open to them, and that the sky can truly be the limit.

When you fire up your grandchildren's imagination and desire to know more, you're giving them a sense of their own promise and potential. Above all, you're showing them that you have faith and believe in them, and that's really the fuel that will keep them going throughout life.

33.

Tell—Don't Show—
That You're Upset

You probably won't make it through a visit with your grandchildren without feeling upset about *something*. You might become frustrated, stressed, or even angry. At these times, you'll probably use every trick you know to try to keep yourself from overreacting to the situation. But it may not always work—sometimes you just have to let off steam. If that happens, you really don't want actions to speak louder than words. The best way to release is to open up and talk about what's upsetting you in as calm a manner as possible.

For a lot of people, this isn't an easy thing to do. Acting out our feelings is often easier than talking about them, but we can also feel much worse afterward for having lost our tempers. When you become less reactive and talk about your negative emotions, you can stop a bad situation from getting worse. This preserves everyone's feelings, including your own. You can control the situation and bring it to a swift and happier conclusion.

Learning to talk first rather than acting is a way to help others relate to you by asking them to put themselves in your place. Suppose you're trying to relax and read quietly, and your grandchildren are playing loudly around you. You've asked them more than once to please take their rambunctious play outside, but they keep disturbing you until you become so frustrated that you're ready to pop. Here's where you pull them aside. Explain that you're upset because you want some quiet time, and they're not honoring what you want. You can ask them how they would feel if they wanted to take a nap and you kept waking them up—probably pretty cranky.

Talking also helps others become aware your feelings. While we all like to think we are caring and considerate of others, we sometimes don't give as much consideration to our own family members. By expressing negative feelings through words rather than actions, you allow your family the chance to understand that they may be stepping on your feelings inadvertently. You can't eradicate anger, frustration, and other upsets from your life entirely. However, you can learn to deal with them in the most peaceful way possible.

34.

Create a Bond to
Span the Miles

The process of building close relationships with your grandchildren means striving to form bonds when you're with them, and finding ways to reinforce those bonds when you're not with them. If you live near your grandchildren, you have plenty of opportunities to bring everyone closer together as a family. But what if you live far away and you are able to see your grandchildren only a few times a year? You have to really take advantage of the time you do have together to create memories that will last over time and across the miles.

It may be a cliché, but it's true: It's the little things that mean the most and will be remembered for years to come. You might remember how you helped your grandmother bake bread and clean up around the house, or how you helped your grandfather rake the yard and wash the car. Often it's the everyday tasks and chores performed together that make wonderful sharing experiences. Let your grandchildren help you with these things. They love to please and help out, so they'll feel very important and mature if you let them assist you with these chores. At the same time, you can all appreciate the moments spent together and perhaps begin to view these ordinary tasks as extraordinary experiences *because* you were together.

Whenever possible, take photos of you and your grandchildren together to record these special times. When you're apart once again, write letters and cards to reminisce about your times together, and enclose a photo with every letter. You might also make a special scrapbook to send to your grandchildren that gives them a view of your daily life when they're not around. Take photos of yourself involved in everyday happenings at home and write about them, or make an audio recording in your own voice. If you go to an exciting show, for example, describe it and enclose the playbill. The purpose is to let your grandchildren "be with you" when they can't be, and get a sense of who you are.

The more you and your grandchildren get to know each other, the more you'll be able to appreciate the time you do spend together and be grateful for those opportunities. The bonds between you will become strong enough to last not only across the miles, but for a lifetime.

35.

Embrace Spontaneity

Children love to do things on the spur of the moment. They'll sometimes shout out ideas for places to go, people to visit, or things to do in such rapid-fire succession that you can't even focus on a single item. They want to run this way and that on a moment's notice. The problem is that a good deal of your life is probably spent planning, following schedules, or doing things according to your appointment book. Kids don't like to hear, "Not now," "Maybe tomorrow," or "Wait until later." If you tell them things like that, you'll probably end up with frustrated grandchildren who can't figure out why you're being stuffy. Let's face it, you might have to get back into a child's frame of mind by embracing their spontaneity and going with the flow.

Spontaneity is ideal to prevent becoming trapped in a rut. Everyone could use a little spontaneity in their lives. How many times have you fallen into the trap of routine, going to the same place each Friday evening, watching the same TV show every

Tuesday night, or eating the same meal every Monday night? It's not that difficult to do. Our routines are familiar, cozy, and unthreatening. But eventually we become bored and unfulfilled. Allow yourself to embrace spontaneity and grab onto the moment. Wonderful times, new memories, and new vital feelings are just ahead, so don't let them pass you by.

You might try looking at your grandchildren's spontaneity in another way. Be pleased and flattered when they think of you in their spontaneous moments. It means you're at the forefront of their thoughts. Besides, no one wants to feel scheduled into a loved one's life. Your grandchildren certainly don't want to be scheduled into yours. Try adopting some of the spontaneous ways of children, and take life as it comes. It's a way to focus your attention on the here and now, rather than fretting about the past or worrying about the future, which can do wonders for relieving stress and anxiety.

36.

Be Open to Learning from
Your Grandchildren

There are many things you teach your grandchildren, but have you ever considered that they might be able to teach you a thing or two? You may understand this concept, but few people are actually open to learning new things from anyone, let alone children. The truth is that children can be our best teachers, and they do this in several ways.

On the practical side, kids can truly teach us some useful things. Are you trying to learn about computers? The whole idea of computers may be frustrating to you, but today's children have grown up with computers, and to many, using a computer is as easy as riding a bicycle was to you. Why not take advantage of that? Your grandchildren want to please you and show off what they know at the same time. Asking them to teach you something is a perfect way for them to do this. You'll learn something useful and acquire a means to relate to your grandchildren on their level, as well.

Grandchildren might also teach you something about yourself. Kids' tendency to speak out and comment on everything from the weather to your behavior may be more than a bit revealing. A testy little voice could actually call your attention to a behavioral quirk that, upon reflection, you may decide could stand some adjustment. Your first tendency may be to be defensive or brush off the comment because it came "from the mouths of babes." But consider that because it came from a child and a fresh viewpoint, it might hold some validity. This isn't to say that everything a child blurts out should be cause for deep reflection, but as with so many things, you can often find pearls amongst the grains of sand.

More importantly, grandchildren can teach you life lessons that they won't even know they're teaching you. Patience, understanding, living in the present moment, considering new ideas, and the all-important concept of unconditional love are just a few of the things you'll learn from your grandchildren through the time you spend together and the experiences you share. The key is to be open to receiving these lessons. You must remember to look for and find the lessons in whatever the experience may be, positive or negative. You can always learn something new. Try letting your grandchildren be your teachers, and see if you don't all feel closer and more loving because of it.

37.

Brag About Them

Grandparents love to brag about their grandchildren, and there's nothing wrong with that. In fact, you *should* brag about them, because they are a great joy in your life, and you're proud of them. Your grandchildren want and need to know that you're proud of them, too. Bragging about them in their presence can go a long way toward boosting their self-esteem.

When the little irritations of family life crop up, it's nice to be reminded that the irritations are temporary. Love, respect, and appreciation for each other are the really important things. If your grandkids are getting on your nerves, you can always think back to a time when they weren't, remember them telling you, "I love you," and move past the problems. Your grandchildren are no different. When family issues involve them, they may feel insecure, wanting and needing to know that you still love them. Knowing that you're proud of them, that you brag about them to your friends, can give them feelings of confidence and security.

When everything is going smoothly, your grandchildren will remember how proud of them you are. Make liberal use of "I love you" with your grandkids—this gives you a winning formula for making them feel good and for feeling good yourself. Don't forget to brag about your children, too. They needed it as kids, and they can probably use some of the same now that they're parents. Use a bit of discretion when bragging—you don't want to overdo it. But when it comes to saying, "I love you," there's no way to ever say it enough.

38.
Learn to Recognize
When They're Bored

Most grandparents dread the times when their grandchildren get all fidgety and agitated and say, "I'm bored!" You've probably tried very hard to have enough things to do so that your grandchildren don't get bored. But that won't always prevent them from being bored, because generally, boredom comes from within ourselves. So if they happen to announce that they're bored, don't immediately rush out to provide them with more amusements. First consider the idea that perhaps it's okay to be bored once in a while and not *have* to be doing something.

Unfortunately, children will probably find this concept very difficult to grasp, and you might, too. We're all so used to being busy. But why don't you try doing absolutely nothing together, and then see what happens? Suggesting this to kids can cause two wildly differing reactions—either they'll stubbornly refuse to try it, or they'll laugh and giggle and give it a shot. If they're resistant, you might try to make a game of it. The idea is to get everyone to sit still and see how long you can do it. Afterward, talk about what happened while you were doing nothing. The first thing you might notice in yourself and the children is that you'll be more relaxed, both physically and mentally. If you've been exercising or active around the house or yard, your body needs a rest to recharge itself before it is ready to go again. Your mind also needs a rest once in a while—doing nothing can provide your mind with much-needed relaxation so it, too, can carry on through the rest of the day. Try it and see if your mind isn't more clear, sharp, and creative.

Another thing to do when grandchildren are bored is to take the opportunity to show them how to use their imaginations to entertain themselves. This can help take the pressure off of you to always be the one to entertain them. In turn, this will keep your grandchildren from always seeking you out to alleviate their boredom. See what ideas they come up with on their own. Ask them what they would like to be doing. If it's something that's not possible to do, why not try daydreaming about the activity together? You can gather up some magazines and cut out photos of things you'd like to do. Or just sit back, relax, and talk about them.

Encourage your grandchildren to avoid the anxiety of always feeling like they have to be doing something—it can promote a more thoughtful relationship between the two of you. And who knows? You might find that some of the best fun you have together actually grows out of being bored.

39.

Make a Scrapbook or
Journal Together

The best things you can share with your grandchildren are often the simplest. One small pleasure is to create and work on a scrapbook together. You can make a record of the children's lives, your life, a family tree, and more. While spending time together, you can pass along stories of family history and lore, giving your grandchildren a true sense of where they come from.

Don't forget the really important benefit of creating a family treasure together—it's a lot of fun! Gather together photos, newspaper clippings, stories you or they may have written down, children's drawings, fingerpaintings, or even kids' favorite pictures from coloring books. Set out a big album, scissors, tape, and glue, and get creative. You might even pull out your camera, the color pencils, or a set of paints to take new photos or make something specifically for the album. There's no limit when it comes to choosing what to include in the book. When everyone's sitting on the floor, making a mess of paper and tape, laughing and sharing wonderful stories, feeling full of love and joy, it somehow becomes difficult for small stuff to interfere.

Without question, creating family treasures together will have lasting value for you and your grandchildren, and these treasures can be part of a legacy passed on to those in future generations. You may never meet your future descendants, but they can still come to know you.

40.

Don't Worry About
What Might Happen

There are few things worse than time and energy wasted on worrying about future incidents that may not come to pass. If you stop and think a moment about how many times you use the word "might," it can be enlightening. A lot of anxiety and stress is generated when your thoughts are constantly sprinkled with "what ifs," particularly where your grandchildren are concerned. If you learn to push such reactive concerns aside and accept each moment as it comes, your life will be more calm and peaceful.

Sometimes parents can be overprotective of their children. Grandparents can behave the same way, even though they may have been through it before with their own children. They know they're overreacting, but can't help themselves. "Sara can't have a bicycle—she *might* get hurt," is one example. This isn't to say that safety isn't an issue when the child rides a bike. Yes, she might get hurt, but we all rode bicycles when we were young, and so did our children. You can't build a protective bubble around the child and insulate her from the world. It's unfair to your granddaughter to deny her the joys and experiences of having her own bicycle because of your worries about what might happen. You can be concerned without being overly worried if you learn to be in the present moment and address such issues from that perspective.

Get your granddaughter a bicycle, but also get her a safety helmet and training wheels. Then take time to help her learn how to ride safely. There is such a thing as healthy concern—that means being reasonably prepared for what could *possibly* happen, but not living your life *expecting* something to befall you, your children, or your grandchildren. Imagine all the moments you will miss if you let your worries get the better of you. Each moment holds the possibility of being special. Pay attention to each moment as it comes, and you will feel how special it is.

41.

Remember What You Loved About *Your* Grandparents

As grandparents, you may encounter times when you become "stuck." You may be looking for the answer to a particular problem. Maybe you don't know how to handle certain situations, or you are at a loss for what to say to your children or grandchildren at a time when you think you must say something. When things like this happen, you may find it comforting to dip into your store of memories and remember what you loved most about your own grandparents.

What made them special to you? Maybe it was how they always had your favorite foods at their home, or because they told you a different bedtime story every night. Maybe it's the way they made you feel when you talked to them. It didn't matter what you said; they hung on to every word. Perhaps it was the skills they had that made you proud because they were so accomplished at them— woodworking, making preserves, sewing, or playing the guitar. You'll probably remember countless instances where they dried your tears, surprised you with little gifts or cards, or simply gave you the biggest hug you can recall. Did they sometimes make mistakes? Probably, but those probably are not what you remember the most. The things you remember most are the things that really count. They are the expressions of love.

That may be the best lesson of all that you learned from your own grandparents. You may not always know the answers to all the problems in your grandchildren's lives or your own, but the truth is that no one does. In the end, your grandchildren will think you're special anyway, not because you could solve the world's problems, but because the little things you did and said could make *any* problems a lot smaller and less important to them.

42.

Special Events Are
Just That: Special

When your grandchildren graduate from school, perform in music or dance recitals, compete in spelling bees, or play important games in sports, they want to share such special events with you. If possible, you should try to attend these events in person so that your grandchildren can see your pride and soak up all of your attention. But if you live too far away or simply can't make the trip for some reason, you can still attend in spirit and show your grandchildren how much you care.

You can always send a card or gift, but why not use your imagination to come up with different, creative ways to share these special moments? You might buy several one-use cameras and mail them to family members to take photos for you. After they use all the film, they can mail the cameras back to you so that you can have the film developed. This way, you'll get plenty of pictures from several different points of view, making sure you've fully covered the whole event. Order multiple copies of the photos, and then send a set to your grandchild with a letter telling how proud you are. You might even put all the photos into an album just for this special event.

Why not sponsor a small party to celebrate the event? You can plan the party over the phone with your grandson and his parents. Discuss inviting a couple of his close friends, along with some family members, and having his favorite foods and music. The only thing you should ask in return is for your grandson to call you during the party so that you can "be there," even for a few minutes, by long-distance.

If you can't be there in person, being there for your grandchildren in spirit can make them feel just as good, because they see that you care enough to make special efforts. As with so many things in life, it's the thought that counts, and such special moments will always be remembered by them and you.

43.

Sometimes, Pretend
They're Not Related to You

As odd as this may sound, you may be able to see your grandchildren—and your children—from a different perspective if you pretend they're not related to you. We're often hardest on the people we love most and, surprisingly, more inclined to give non-relatives a break or the benefit of the doubt. Trying this little experiment can help you to look at your family from a different, perhaps more balanced, point of view.

Sometimes grandparents can become overly critical of their children or grandchildren just *because* they are theirs. They can have greater expectations of them than they do of others, and do not necessarily see their loved ones as they really are. For example, you may criticize your granddaughter's choice of friends or a direction she's taking in school. There may be nothing wrong in either situation—you may simply have had different expectations. If you pretend for a moment that your granddaughter isn't yours, how do these situations look? You may find that she seems to be a normal kid with normal friends who is making normal choices. If you wouldn't criticize these choices when made by another child, why be so hard on your own family?

This strategy can be especially good in times of conflict or stress. In a way, pretending your grandkids aren't related to you can put some distance between you and the conflict. Suppose your grandson runs up your long-distance telephone bill each time he visits you, because he's calling his friends back home. This irritates and upsets you—the money might not matter, but you feel as if he's taking advantage of you, overdoing it with your phone without even asking you. Or maybe the money does matter, especially if you're on a fixed income. But to keep the peace and not upset the rest of the family, you don't say anything to him or his parents. You keep it inside and get stressed out each time he does it again. Now, try pretending that he's not related to you and ask yourself: If he were the grandson of one of my friends, and he were treating my friend—or me—this way, what would I do? Looking at it from this different perspective, you would probably urge your friend to put a stop to the situation—maybe even chide your friend for not taking action earlier. With this new perspective, don't you think it may be time for you to speak up and take away your stress and irritation? This type of talk may be best held in a private, one-on-one conversation between you and your grandson. You can explain to him how you feel and what you would like him to do.

We all need a fresh perspective on life now and then. Sometimes taking a different view of those closest to us is all that's needed to put things back in perspective.

44.

Don't Always Make Them
Color Inside the Lines

Imagine what the world would be like if each and every person looked alike, sounded the same, did everything perfectly, and believed exactly the same things. Boring doesn't even begin to describe it. The richness and beauty of this earth and its people come from vast diversity, whether it's the extremes of climate from one region to another, the different cultures of nations on opposite sides of the globe, or the uniqueness of each individual person.

Your grandchildren, too, are unique individuals, growing and developing their own ideas, thoughts, tastes, and viewpoints. As individuals, they may not always see things in the same way that you do. In fact, there may be times when they don't follow the crowd at all, marching to the beat of their own drum. This isn't a bad thing. In fact, the principle of separate realities—that individual people are vastly different from one another—says that it can be no other way. Recognizing and appreciating your grandchildren's individuality, and even encouraging it, can greatly increase your understanding and tolerance of anyone who holds ideas and beliefs different from yours.

Remember that some of the greatest discoveries and creations in science, art, medicine, and literature came from people who didn't "color inside the lines," so to speak. If your grandchildren want to explore a bit, perhaps color outside the lines, let them. It's a loving thing to be accepting, even relishing the great individuality of each grandchild. That understanding and compassion can bring you even closer together. Seeing what is wonderful and unique about each person can help you see and appreciate your own uniqueness, as well.

45.

If You Talk, They Will Listen— but Do It at Bedtime

It can be difficult to have a good talk with kids. There are so many external things to distract them from really listening to you—television, toys, friends, pets, even food and drink. During the day, there's always something stimulating them and grabbing their attention. You, on the other hand, can probably grab it and hold it only in short bursts. Trying to have any kind of meaningful conversation with children when their thoughts are scattered all over the place can be frustrating for you and for them. It's not that your grandchildren don't want to or can't listen to you. They will listen, but if you want to really focus their attention, try having one-on-one discussions at bedtime.

Bedtime is when everyone is usually calm and relaxed. Most people tend to be reflective and really think about things while lying in bed after turning out the lights but before falling asleep. There are no distractions. The TV is quiet, the phone is (hopefully) not ringing, and you're relaxed and can concentrate more easily. If you think about it, bedtime is often when some of the best, most meaningful conversations happen between adults for the same reason: lack of external distractions.

Unless kids are extremely sleepy and nodding off, use this time to sit and discuss anything they—or you—want to talk about. From smaller children to teenagers, sitting down on the bed to chat is a very informal way to connect with kids. You can tell stories or chat about the family. If you confide in them (yes, tell them little secrets), they will be encouraged to confide in you. If everyone is really relaxed and feeling good, you might broach touchy or problem subjects at this time, as well, just between you and the child. You may find that the closeness and calm environment can do wonders to make such discussions far easier. To keep the flow of conversation going, be sure to give kids your full attention when they have something to say. As they open up to you, be truly sympathetic, and don't criticize or discount their feelings by saying things like, "Oh, you shouldn't get so upset," or "It will all be better tomorrow."

The best part about chatting at bedtime, especially if you're covering some problem areas, is that you can all get things off your chest, and everyone can go to bed feeling much better and more peaceful. Before you turn out the lights, don't forget to kiss them good-night and to say, "I love you."

46.

Share Their World

Children live in the now, and they grow and change every day.
For grandparents who aren't involved in their grandchildren's
lives on a day-to-day basis, it can almost be like meeting new people
each time you visit with them! Their likes and dislikes seem to
change overnight. They acquire new tastes in music, clothes, and
friends. Sometimes you feel that you can't keep up with them. That's
why it's so important for grandparents to share their grandchildren's
world. It is one way to really know and appreciate each other.

Sharing their world can be easier than you might think. Take
time to visit their school during open house, or fill in for a parent and
take her to a dentist appointment. Have lunch with him and a couple
of his friends, or do a project on the computer together. Attend a
sporting event together, or grab a bowl of popcorn and sit down to
watch cartoons with them. The more you learn and participate in
their world, the stronger the bond between you becomes.

An interesting way to share their world is to invite them to share yours. Call it an intergeneration "cultural exchange": You and your grandchildren make a deal to exchange knowledge and experiences from each other's worlds. Have you ever noticed that the generation gap is always the widest when music is playing—theirs and yours? Try learning about each other's favorite music by making an exchange. Agree to sit and listen to some of your granddaughter's favorite songs with her *if* she will sit and listen to some of *your* favorite songs with you. Likewise, you can trade dance steps with her, do a movie exchange, a book exchange, or even a shopping exchange. Time spent together in this way can lead to greater understanding all around, and help form bonds that span time and distance.

So open your mind and heart, and get ready to enter the unique world of your grandchildren. Don't forget to invite them to share your world, too.

47.

Remember That You Have
Something in Common—
Their Parents

There's an old saying that grandchildren and grandparents get along so well because they have a common enemy: the parents. Unfortunately, believing in this negative myth can cause a lot of problems in families by opening generation gaps even wider. Wouldn't it be more loving to say that grandparents and grandchildren get along because they have a common love?

Often grandparents act as a buffer in conflicts between their children and grandchildren, particularly when older children are involved. Encouraging the idea of a common love can help smooth these sometimes rocky family relationships. It can be quite easy to say, "We're all working toward the same goal here—you love your parents and we love your parents, so let's talk." The important thing is to keep your perspective and distance from the problems while guiding everyone to see each other's viewpoints. You don't want to take sides with either your children or your grandchildren, nor do you want either of them to see you as the final solution to the problem. Rather, act as the peacekeeper, and use some very unique knowledge that only you hold: You know your children better than their own children do. Armed with this, you can encourage understanding all around.

Think back to a time when your children were young and the same problem may have occurred. You can relate this story to your grandchildren to show them that their parents went through the same growing pains and struggles that they are experiencing. It may help the children to gain more understanding of their parents—they will realize that what their parents have to say often comes from their own experience, not just from thin air. So if children are tempted to think that their parents don't understand them, they may find that they actually understand them all too well.

Offer your support to your children, and remind them of how the situation was handled in the past. One way or another, there were lessons to be learned, and those lessons could help smooth over any potential family conflicts. Remind your children, too, that they are the common love between you all.

48.

Your Grandchildren Are Not
Just Like Your Children

Watching your grandchildren can sometimes be like stepping into a time machine. For just a moment, you can almost believe you're watching your own children at that age again. You might see it in their faces, their mannerisms, or maybe even the sounds of their voices. It can bring back the most wonderful memories and warm feelings.

It's natural to see your children in your grandchildren, and you may even look for a little bit of yourself in them. That's okay, as long as you always remember that your grandchildren are individuals with unique personalities, interests, goals, and desires. While they may look and act like their parents, they are not exactly like them, so let your grandchildren be themselves. This becomes especially crucial with older children who begin to consider their lives' directions and choose career paths. It's not uncommon in some families to have expectations that a child will be "just like his father" or "just like her mother" by attending the same college or choosing the same career. Some grandparents might even expect that everyone will join the family business or follow the family tradition of being next in a long line of doctors, lawyers, teachers, or nurses. This can place a tremendous amount of pressure on grandchildren who may have no desire to follow in a parent's or grandparent's footsteps. Even more importantly, their talents may not lie in the same areas. All of the pressure and expectations can cause conflict and hurt feelings in the family.

Grandparents can support and motivate grandchildren to follow their own paths. Resist the urge to tell them that they should do certain things "because your parents did that at your age." Honor their choices, and show genuine enthusiasm for their interests and desires. Rather than forcing your grandchildren to live in their parents' shadows or mirror their parents' accomplishments, encourage them to follow their own hearts. In this way, they will make decisions in life based on their own values rather than society's or their family's expectations. When any person tries to live life according to the expectations of others instead of following the voice from within, that person is in constant struggle with the self, living a life of frustration and great stress. Peace from within comes from doing with your life what your heart tells you to do, even if it takes you down a different path from the one that others think you should follow.

It's fun to see and enjoy the similarities between your children and your grandchildren, but it's important to accept and relish their differences. Recognizing your grandchildren's individuality will truly make them feel loved and cherished, and that's exactly how you want them to feel.

49.

Take Care of Their Minds

Recently, there has been a strong push to promote physical fitness in young people. But it's equally important to take care of their minds. Just as the body needs a workout to grow fit and strong, so does the mind need to be exercised and challenged. Becoming knowledgeable about current events and the world around you is an important way to become a more understanding and accepting person. This is a good cause for grandparents to take up, since grandchildren often look more to them for wisdom and knowledge than they do their own parents.

Grandparents can encourage grandchildren to explore and learn by offering them the opportunities. The bonus is that you can keep your own mind challenged and working, as well. When considering activities to do together, be sure to include museums, exhibits, libraries, and other outlets for stimulating and challenging their minds. Most importantly, encourage them to be open to new ideas and the thoughts and opinions of others. Children must learn to be tolerant of other people's differing philosophies and opinions. Encourage them to learn from people who think differently from the way that they do. Explain to them that this will broaden their perspective, and that we don't always have to turn people around to our own point of view. Grasping this concept will serve them well throughout their lives. Encourage them to read books with opposing points of view. This can show them that there are two sides to everything, and possibly more than two. By accepting and appreciating the fact that not everyone thinks alike, they can learn tolerance and acceptance of others.

It can be interesting and fun to actually challenge some stereotypes or preconceived ideas together. Why not have Grandma take the kids to a baseball game, or have Grandpa take them shopping for clothes? Challenging and broadening the mind allows us to see the big picture, rather than spending our energy sweating the small stuff.

50.

Take Care of Their Bodies

Physical activity is so important for young people, yet today, many of them aren't getting nearly enough. Kids have a lot of diversions—computers, television, and video games—that keep them rooted in a chair instead of moving about and getting exercise. The real shame is that kids are more overweight today than ever before, and the problem seems to be getting worse. This hurts them physically and mentally. Overweight children often suffer from lack of self-esteem. Today's schoolyards have no shortage of bullies to remind kids of things like their size, weight, or appearance.

One of the best things you can do for your grandchildren is to encourage them to take care of themselves physically. You can teach them to be healthy by example, of course, and that helps you maintain yourself, as well. You don't have to become a health and fitness nut to stay healthy, but paying attention to your health can be a shared interest that helps make your relationship with your grandchildren extra-special. Your new commitment doesn't have to be an exclusive club, either. Share your interest with their parents, too, and bring the whole family closer by working toward a common goal.

Getting started isn't easy, but it's more fun when everyone gets involved. Trade books, articles, and other information on fitness topics that interest all of you. Plan healthy meals together, and learn to cook more healthily by experimenting with recipes together. Try new and different fitness activities to find one or more that you all enjoy and can do together. You might try walking, biking, swimming—even horseback riding or skiing. The important thing is to make a commitment to being healthy, not just for yourself, but for each other. The truth is that members of loving families can give each other no greater gift than to be healthy and at their best for each other.

Healthy bodies—theirs and yours—translate to healthy, more relaxed, and more peaceful minds. When you feel well, problems and troubles just don't seem quite as big.

51.

Learn to Lose Your
Hearing on Occasion

Though this strategy can be applied to any type of pesky noise, it's particularly effective when you have kids in the household. Sometimes you just need to tune out so that the little irritations don't bother you. In other words, lose your hearing when your grandchildren are complaining, fighting with each other, or causing a general ruckus.

At first, you may think that this is ignoring bad behavior, and therefore condoning it. But what you're really trying to do is alter your reactions to their behavior, and in turn alter their behavior. For example, if every time your grandchildren get noisy and rambunctious, your first reaction is to immediately stop whatever you're doing and get into an exchange with them, they will learn that this kind of loud behavior is a good way to get your attention.

Try losing your hearing, and see what happens. It may be difficult to tune out at first, but with practice, you'll find it becomes easier. You are learning to give yourself a break, so to speak, and are using these few moments to regroup without reacting right away. You can actually change your habit of immediately getting upset and frustrated into a chance to reflect upon your own thoughts and feelings. Not only are you changing your reactive habits, you are also influencing the behavioral habits of your grandchildren. If you lose your hearing, they may simply give up their unruly behavior or fighting on their own. Your stress level will be much lower, and so will theirs. Then the possibility of enjoying each other's company can once again become a reality.

52.

Turn the TV Off

Isn't it funny how in this advanced age of communications and entertainment, with over 100 channels of television available, there can still be nothing worth watching? On the other hand, having 100 books always insures that there is something to read. In the days before television, family life was centered on the home and being together. Reading books, storytelling, playing games, and talking are all things we can do with the TV turned off. These activities can bring us closer together, expand our minds, reduce the stresses of everyday life, and make us more loving.

Television does have some redeeming qualities. In fact, TV has come a long way as far as offering quality programming, and there are plenty of fascinating, entertaining, and educational shows to watch. TV can even be an activity to share with your grand-children if you sit down to watch a favorite show together. The problem is that many people put too much emphasis on television, and they incorporate it into too many areas of their lives, often without realizing it. We can read the paper in the morning, eat meals, get dressed, clean house, do homework, even talk on the phone—all at the same time the TV is continuously playing in the background. Parents and grandparents sometimes use TV as a baby-sitter—they just turn it on and sit the kids down in front of it. We get used to that background noise, and don't remember what quiet sounds like.

It's time to turn off the tube. Gather up your grandchildren, and do something for your minds, bodies, and souls. Kids can be easily distracted, which means you can take their attention away from TV, too. They live in the moment, and if they protest at first, they'll get over it very quickly and turn their attention to what you're doing instead. Read a book together, take a walk in the woods, go bird watching, play a game, draw pictures, or color in a coloring book. The list of things you can do when you hit that off button is endless. Just remember that the idea of this strategy is not to tune out television forever, but to realize that there's more to life than what comes over the airwaves, and that a little peace and quiet can be a welcome change for everyone.

53.

The Answer to "Why?"
Is Not "Because"

Children can sometimes drive you crazy with questions about this and that, as their hungry little minds seek knowledge about the world around them. It seems that the most common question kids can ask is, "Why?" Since children view their grandparents as great sources of wisdom and knowledge, it's natural that they're going to bombard you with all kinds of questions, especially the whys.

Kids want to know why things work the way they do, why people do the things they do, why you said something you said—and on and on. "Why is the sky blue? Why is the grass green? Why don't dogs walk on their hind legs the way people do?" Take a moment to look at these questions, and see them from a child's point of view. You might remember how mysterious such simple things were to you when you were a child, or what it was like when your own children peppered you with whys. You might also remember how disappointed you (or they) felt if the answer was, "Because." Children can feel hurt and brushed off by that stock adult answer. To them, this means that someone they trust won't take the time or make the effort to answer their questions. Often kids will persist in trying to get an answer, becoming quite frustrated and upset if they don't get one that satisfies them more than "Because."

Taking the time to feed your grandchildren's hungry minds is important. If you need to think about the question for a moment, then you can work up a good answer, sit down, and have a little discussion about it. In some cases, the answers to their questions might be too complicated for them to understand, or the subject matter too mature to broach. If that happens, you might say to your grandchildren, "I'd love to talk about that with you now, but I'll have to tell you when you're a little older. You'll be able to understand then." There's nothing wrong with telling kids that sometimes in life, you have to wait for things.

The fact is that you may not know the answer to your grandchildren's questions. If that's the case, be honest and tell them that you don't know. Suggest that you research the answer together. Take your grandchildren to the library, look in an encyclopedia, surf the Internet, or ask an expert. Seek out the answer as soon as you can find the time together. Don't put it off so long that you forget about it. Your grandchildren will always remember that you took them seriously and took the time to help them learn.

54.

Get to Know
Your Neighbor's Kids

This strategy can serve many purposes and help keep life from becoming overwhelming on several fronts. If you don't see your grandchildren very often, you may get out of the habit of having kids around. When they do visit again, getting back into the swing of things may take a bit of time. But if you get to know your neighbor's children, it can help you keep in contact with kids on a regular basis. With exposure to children, how they talk, the way they dress, and their hobbies and interests, you'll keep up to date and be able to relate better to your grandchildren whenever you do spend time together. Plus you might gain some extra insight into your own grandchildren.

Your grandchildren can always benefit from making new friends, and so can you. When you know the local children, you can invite them to meet your grandchildren when they come to visit. Expanding your grandchildren's circles of friends by helping them make friends away from home can give them a broader perspective on life. Suppose your grandchildren are growing up in a big city, but you live in the country. Becoming friends with some country kids will introduce them to new experiences and help your grandkids to appreciate children whose lives are different from theirs. Having their own friends near you can also add to their enjoyment when they come to visit you—and you can get a break during that time, as well.

Anything you can do to promote living in harmony—whether within your family or your neighborhood—is worth trying. Becoming closer to your neighbors and their families will only enhance your relationships with your own grandchildren and infuse your lonely times with hope and happiness.

55.

Explain Yourself—Often

A common problem in families is a tendency to "shut down" and not communicate problems to one another. If something is weighing heavily on your mind, it surely won't go unnoticed by those around you. If you don't share what's burdening you, the rest of the family is left to make their own interpretations. They might begin to draw conclusions on their own, and that's fertile ground for frustration to take root and grow. After all, your family can't read your mind.

Share what's troubling you—it will help keep frustration levels down and allow others a chance to help you, too. It also prevents your concerns and problems from building up to a high-pressure point. You certainly don't want to become overly reactive and get so stressed that you can't keep yourself from losing your temper. If you do, you'll probably feel awful—not to mention how everyone else in the family will feel. For this reason, it's especially important to somehow clue in your grandchildren to your thoughts and moods so that they don't mistakenly think they've done something to upset you. If you can learn to be open and honest about your feelings, it leaves little room for misinterpretation.

Think about how you try to encourage your grandchildren to tell you what's bothering them or talk about what makes them feel bad. When they do talk to you about it, the process seems to magically make the problems either diminish or disappear. Sharing your problems and emotions removes your burden, as does knowing that someone cares enough to want to help. Love and compassion make life seem brighter. If you can help others in that way, why not let them feel good about helping you, too? You'll be surprised at how quickly your problems can go away and be replaced by loving feelings from your family.

56.

Create a Passion for Giving

It can be wonderful for families to get involved in charity work. Giving of time, material things, or money is rewarding and fun when you do it together with a real passion for giving and making a difference. There's no better time than when children are young to get them into the spirit and the habit of giving.

Finding a cause or charity to work with is the first step that you can all take together. Have a family team meeting specifically to discuss potential projects. In doing so, you can introduce your grandchildren to the fact that the world is filled with those less fortunate than they are. Talk about homelessness, poverty, hunger, and the special problems of children and the elderly. Or discuss homeless animals, local wildlife and nature conservation projects, or community projects such as building more playgrounds for children. This time of discovery will help you learn what interests or excites your grandchildren. Then you can gather more information about those areas and learn what you can do to help.

Whatever you choose to do, make it a family project. Together, you can go through closets looking for good clothing that you simply don't wear anymore, or items you no longer use that someone in need can appreciate. Bag and box the items, and then go together to a local charity or church and donate them.

Holidays are the perfect time to develop the spirit and passion for giving. Churches, homeless shelters, and food banks often need volunteers at holiday time to help serve meals to the homeless and disadvantaged. A few hours spent volunteering together in this way can introduce a whole new perspective on giving thanks. It doesn't matter whether your causes are national, international, or local, whether you write a check or pitch in to volunteer your time—the key is for the whole family to become involved and embrace the spirit of giving.

Just as important as giving is the concept of giving without expecting anything in return, including recognition. Find ways to give something anonymously. Your grandchildren can learn that there's no need for recognition—the good feelings they'll get from giving to others will last them for a long time.

57.

Take a Walk

One of the best ways to become a more relaxed and peaceful person is to make walking a regular part of your life. Of course, you walk quite a bit every day, usually for some specific reason and as a form of transportation. But there is more to walking than just moving from one place to another.

In his book *Full Catastrophe Living*, author Jon Kabat-Zinn describes a form of walking called "walking meditation." This simply means walking and paying attention to the actual experience of walking, being fully aware of what an incredible feat your feet are performing! It means walking without having a specific place to go, walking simply for the sake of walking—and paying attention to the experience. When life gets a bit chaotic and you're feeling stressed, try ten minutes of walking meditation to calm your mind and soothe your nerves.

You can also walk with the desire to pay more attention to the world around you—there's nothing like the grandeur of nature.

This is an experience you can also share with your children and grandchildren. Take them on a walking tour without headphones or cell phones. Allow only the desired distractions to take your attention: nature, each other, and people you might meet and greet along the way.

Your neighbor's orange tabby cat might say hello to you all. You'll feel a breeze that carries the scent of freshly baked bread from the deli a few blocks away. The blue blossoms of a jacaranda bush flowing over a garden wall will amaze you. There is so much to see and experience, and you can do it all at a calm, relaxed pace when you take your family for a walk. It's a special time together to share thoughts, ideas, and wonderful sights. The best part is that it's free and always available. Try it and see if you and your family don't become hooked on walking—and a lot more relaxed because of it.

58.

Play to Your Grandchildren's Strengths
and Accept Their Weaknesses

People have strengths in certain areas and weaknesses in others—that's how life is. No one can do everything well, nor should anyone be expected to do so. Learning to recognize where people's strengths and weaknesses lie can help you relate to them in a more tolerant and understanding manner.

Like everyone else, your grandchildren will be better at some things than others. If you develop your ability to see their strengths and weaknesses, you won't have expectations of them that are unrealistic. Suppose you're a dyed-in-the-wool football fan. You would love for your grandson to play football, but athletics just aren't where his strengths and talents lie. It won't do either of you any good to push him into trying out for the football team. If he doesn't want to, but feels forced to do it in order to please you, he'll feel strong resentments that will cloud your relationship. Besides that, he could get physically hurt if he's getting into a game of strength at which he's not very good. You may be disappointed that your grandson won't become a football player, but try to focus instead on what strengths he does have. Maybe he's good at art, music, or building things with his hands. Wherever his talents lie, if he really enjoys something, encourage him in that direction and praise his accomplishments. Support him, or involve yourself in his interests, and enjoy the quality time alone together. Most importantly, you're showing your grandson that you accept him for who he is and that what he wants in life matters to you.

This is an important strategy to remember for everyone in your family. By playing to people's strengths and accepting their weaknesses, you encourage them to live their lives in a manner that is true for them, rather than trying to put them into your own idea of how they should live. Living from the heart is what we should all strive for. You can accept life for what it is, and enjoy it more than if you're in a constant struggle with how you wish life was.

59.

Put Away Your Watch

How often do you look at your watch or a clock on the wall, say, "I have to go!" and rush off to wherever it is you're going? Or maybe when you're wrapped up in a project, suddenly you notice that time has slipped by, and you panic because you weren't paying close attention to the time. Some people live lives dictated by the clock. Of course, if you're a working person with a schedule, and you have to be at work or appointments at specific times, then living by a clock—at least during work hours—is important. But how many other times in your life do you allow the clock to rule you, when indeed it may not be necessary at all?

A timepiece can be a stern master—one that may chide you and force you to obey. Grandparents looking to spend quality time with their grandchildren would do well to put away their watches whenever possible. When you're with kids, time spent paying attention to your watch could be time spent paying attention to them. Remember the three things your grandchildren want most from you: attention, attention, and attention! If they see you giving more attention to your watch, they will feel that something or someone else is more important than they are. This is probably not the message you want to give them.

This isn't to say that scheduled events like doctor appointments should be missed. In fact, those things are easily explained to grandchildren and likely understood by them. The idea is to learn to discern what's necessary and demanding of your time and what isn't in the context of your family. The fact is that you may be able to put off or reschedule a number of things that cause you to look at your watch. A favorite TV show can always be taped and watched at another time. Even a regular card game with your friends can be missed once in a while.

The next time you find yourself constantly checking your watch, ask yourself, "Is the reason that I'm looking at my watch worth it? Is there something that's absolutely necessary for me to do, or is it something minor that I can cancel or postpone?" Make that decision carefully, and be truly happy with your choice. Sometimes we need to stand knee-deep in the flow of life and simply go wherever it takes us. At times like these, and especially when your grandchildren are around, a watch isn't really necessary.

60.

Be Aware of
Your Mood Hints

Moods are funny things. They come and go, day in and day out, often several times a day, all the time. Even the calmest, coolest people can have times when a good mood will switch to a low mood. Some people have a more difficult time with their moods and wear them rather prominently as they go from one extreme to the other. You know people like that—they're often described as colorful, volatile, temperamental, and mercurial.

When moods change, our perceptions of life and the people close to us can change, as well. Think of it as looking through the proverbial rose-colored glasses one minute and then taking them off the next. The world around you can look pretty different. What satisfies us and makes us happy during a good mood may disturb or bore us when in a bad mood. Such ups and downs can be difficult on the people around us. We can find ourselves getting caught on the roller-coaster ride of our loved ones' moods.

It can pay to learn to recognize your own "mood hints," the little hints your low or angry moods can give you when they're about to make appearances. Like a storm announces its approach with thunder, lightning, and gathering dark clouds, a bad or angry mood rarely appears suddenly, without notice. You can generally feel the onset of a foul mood due to stress, a headache, some bad luck, the phone constantly ringing—any number of irritations. But if you do recognize your mood hints, what next? You can't always fend off the bad mood whenever you feel it coming on, though it's wonderful if you can find a way to do that. Sometimes you simply have to ride it out. What you can do, however, is know that when your bad mood hits, you are likely to see things a lot differently. This is the part that can lead to unpleasant consequences for your loved ones if you're not careful.

Suppose you're in a low mood and trying to complete a project, and your grandchildren are trying very hard to get your attention. During a good mood, you might shoo them off with a laugh or perhaps let them help you. But in a bad mood, you could become short-tempered and yell at them.

Learning to recognize your mood hints and knowing that your moods can color your view of the world can help you avoid taking the low moods so seriously. You may also be able to take steps to insulate your loved ones from a low mood until it passes. Take a walk to relieve stress, hang a "Do Not Disturb" sign on the door to your den and spend some time alone, or relax for a bit with a good book. You might try deep breathing, relaxation exercises, or ten minutes of yoga. It's not a bad thing to want some solitude now and then. In families that are aware of each other's needs, seeking time alone is understood and can be done without hurting any feelings. Whatever you do, your mood hints can help make your low moments more manageable and keep the peace at home.

61.

Embrace the
"Full Catastrophe"

Sometimes life presents you with one challenge after another. Your best-laid plans for a favorite activity with your whole family suddenly go awry, followed by the kitchen faucet springing a leak and turning into a geyser. After weeks of anticipating your granddaughter's visit, she and her parents arrive, and she promptly comes down with the flu, which soon spreads to her parents. Even the weather won't necessarily cooperate. In the midst of the chaos that family life can sometimes become, what else can you do except grab the baton and run with it?

The title of John Kabat-Zinn's book *Full Catastrophe Living* is paraphrased from a line in the novel *Zorba the Greek*: "Of course I've been married. Wife, house, kids, everything...the whole catastrophe!" He's certainly not implying that family life is a catastrophe—rather, the phrase is meant in happy appreciation for the richness of life, from good to bad. Zorba's way, says Kabat-Zinn, "is to 'dance' in the gale of the full catastrophe, to celebrate life, to laugh with it and at himself, even in the face of personal failure and defeat. In doing so, he is never weighed down for long." It appears that the famous Zorba has learned to not sweat the small stuff.

In the midst of your own "full catastrophe," you can get frustrated and angry, of course, but that will only make things worse. Negative emotions aren't going to help. What can help is to remember that the full catastrophe means that life is full of good times and bad, and that eventually, both will pass. Nothing lasts forever, and everything is in a state of constant change. Another experience will occur, and you never know just what it will be. Rather than become upset or fight the problems, accept that this is simply how life is, and embrace it all. The very best moment to be in is the one you're in right now. You can anguish over the past and wring your hands in anxiety about the future. But if you think about how much precious time and energy is wasted in that way, you'll find that the present, from one moment to the next, never seems quite as bad.

When life is calm, it's easy to love the full catastrophe. The real challenge is to stop in the middle of chaos, look at your children and grandchildren, remember the good times, and ask yourself honestly: Would you really want it any other way?

62.

Remember That Tears
Aren't Always Bad

The flow of life isn't always in one direction. Things never go just one way. Along with the good times, we learn to take the bad. With grandchildren, the happy times are intermingled with times of tears, and those times can often be difficult for loving parents and grandparents to take.

Adults often demand that children stop crying and sometimes get angry when they don't. Shouting at a child to stop crying is a guarantee of more crying—and the more kids cry, the angrier adults can get. Children crying can indeed be an irritation, but it's inevitable. Children cry, and it's not always bad. Learning to accept that and relate differently to crying can make you less reactive and more compassionate when it happens. When children cry, it's comfort they want and need, not angry words or actions.

Crying is how children express their emotions if they become upset, or how they express physical pain if they somehow get hurt.

It's a natural release, yet children are often given mixed messages about crying. They are told that "big boys don't cry," or are admonished to "be a big girl and stop crying." This implies that it's adult to hold your emotions inside. We forget that children can see their grandfathers get choked up when recalling war experiences or see their grandmothers begin to cry when thinking about loved ones who are no longer with them. In fact, they can see people crying from happiness at weddings or graduation ceremonies. Emotions ranging from pure joy to total rage to deep sorrow can naturally be accompanied by crying, even in the most mature adults. So when kids cry and adults get angry at them, the messages confuse them.

Crying isn't something to discourage all of the time. However, this doesn't mean that you simply let a child cry and ignore him. Rather, crying should be comforted and shared. Be compassionate—take the chance to share your grandson's sad experience, whatever it is. Encourage him to talk about the emotions behind the crying. Often adults may try to stop a child's crying simply because they don't want to deal with whatever is making the child cry.

If you stop to think about it, anger provoked by a child's tears is more likely anger at the situation that caused it. Becoming less reactive in general can make it easier to relate to a child's crying, especially if you don't fight it and remember that it will pass very quickly. It can take much more effort to be angry and frustrated for a minute than it does to be understanding, compassionate, and comforting for the same length of time. Which do you think your grandchildren will appreciate more in the long run?

Some of the happiest people around will admit that sometimes they cry, too. If you can learn to accept crying as a normal, passing emotion in your grandchildren, you will be able to handle it.

63.

Learn to Screen
the "I Want's"

Wanting things without restriction can end up making contentment and happiness unreachable goals. If children can learn this lesson, their lives will be far less stressful and frustrating. Grandparents are ideal teachers to convey this wisdom, because they are often the target of the perpetual "I want's."

Kids can come to think of grandparents as a never-ending source of "things." There's nothing wrong with indulging them every now and then, perhaps spoiling them a little. But responding to *all* of their "I want's" can do two things: First, it can lead to more and more "I want's." Kids can get caught up in a cycle of wanting more, bigger, better—and adults are just as susceptible to this notion, if not more so. It seems that satisfaction never comes, because once you get what you want, you immediately want something else. You actually take little time to enjoy what you've acquired before your thoughts turn, once again, to what you want next. Children can very easily fall into this pattern of wanting material things. Or worse, they can become demanding, wanting their desires to be met instantly. "I want to go to the movies!" "I want to eat dinner *right now!*" Their wants can get completely out of hand.

The second thing that giving in to all the "I want's" can do is remove all special meaning from your giving. A rich man once explained why he ate his favorite caviar only on his birthday, even though he could afford to have it every day: "If I had it every day, it wouldn't be special anymore." Answering all of the "I want's" can make it nearly impossible to make a birthday special, for example. A gift from grandparents will not hold any special meaning—it's just another "thing." Imagine how stressful and disappointing life will be for a child who reaches that point at a young age.

Remember that the advertising messages to which children are exposed are constantly telling them that they must have more. When they say "I want" all of the time, they are responding to that. Grandparents can counteract the messages by using their judgement to screen the "I want's," rather than giving in to every one of them. The message to go along with that action is to be happy with what you have now. Happiness can be chased and chased—and never caught—if you always see it as being somewhere up ahead of you.

If the "I want's" come at holiday time, you might also turn your grandchildren's attention to the act of giving. Find a charity to support. Then teach the kids about what others need, and contrast it to what they want. Show them how good they can feel by helping or giving to someone in need. In the end, you're showing that happiness doesn't come from "things" after all, but rather from what you feel inside.

64.

Learn to "Chill Out"

You may have heard someone tell a stressed person to "chill out," meaning calm down, take a breather, and let your stress subside. Whenever you're feeling a bit overwhelmed, you might try to literally chill out—that is, learn to cool down and relax with a simple meditation technique that involves deep breathing, counting, and feeling a cool breeze soothe and calm you.

It's pretty simple. The next time you feel yourself getting angry, tense, or stressed, take a long, deep breath, close your eyes if possible, and say the word "one" to yourself. You can speak it softly or say it in your mind. At the same time, try to see the word "one" or the numeral "1" in your mind. Next, release your breath, and relax your muscles. As you continue with the number "two," try to feel a nice, cool breeze blowing across your arms, your face, and your neck. You might remember a time of great relaxation when a cool breeze blowing over your body was part of the experience— perhaps a vacation you took, or a weekend trip to the beach.

Remember the feeling of that wonderful breeze, how it calmed and soothed your mind and your frazzled nerves. Feel that breeze again as you continue your counting to ten.

If you've been really upset, you may need to count past ten. But this process of breathing, counting, and visualizing can make it nearly impossible to stay stressed. Increasing oxygen to your brain, slowing down your breathing, and relaxing your heart rate will bring an overall calm to your body. When you finish, you should be relaxed and able to look at your stresses with a different perspective.

People who practice this form of mini-meditation say that they can eventually call up the cool breeze on a moment's notice and chill out under most any circumstances. Give it a try, and here's a suggestion: Don't limit "chilling out" to times when you're stressed or angry. A daily dose of meditation can chase away irritations and make peace and calm a routine part of your life.

65.

Take Care of Their Spirits

Children are quite curious about spiritual matters. They want to know who God is, where heaven is located, if the uncle or aunt who died last year is there, if God likes baseball—and on and on. Kids see their grandparents as a source of wisdom and knowledge, and often take such spiritual questions to them. Grandparents can nurture their grandchildren's spiritual sides by taking time to address their questions and letting them know that their concerns are important.

Too often, children are brushed off in their spiritual quests, or embarrassed into silence by other children who tease them and label their questions stupid or dumb. On the contrary, grandparents can point out how wonderful it is to be inquisitive about the universe and your place in it. Make it a point to give your full attention to your grandchildren's explorations of spirit, and assure them that their questions are valid and worth discussing.

Nurturing of spirit begins with your teaching values and beliefs by example. But what if your own spirit needs a little nurturing? You and your grandchildren can explore these matters together. We are reminded by the world's great spiritual leaders to constantly seek what is holy in the world around us and in the everyday things of life. We are to look not only at the beauty of the flowers and the trees, the sunrise and the sea, but at the not-so-beautiful things that are also the wonderful handiwork of God. You and your grandchildren can explore lessons to be learned from poverty, sickness, or tragedy. Is there beauty in that which at first appears to be ugly? Consider the story of the caterpillar and the butterfly. Who would think that a creepy, spiky little worm could turn into such a magnificent creature? All things hold in them the potential for beauty of some kind. When we learn to tune into that beauty, we become more grateful and loving inside.

Your grandchildren's spiritual lives may be of great concern to you, and you may want to discuss with your children any conflicting beliefs or boundaries they may wish to set. No matter what the situation, the best way for grandparents to attend to their grandchildren's spiritual needs is by being living examples of spiritual peace, harmony, and gratitude.

66.

Cultivate Understanding—
Yours and Theirs

Better, more loving relationships of any kind start and grow within a climate of understanding. This means becoming genuinely interested in understanding others, rather than trying so hard to have others understand you. So often, lack of true understanding is the cause of friction and conflict in families, especially between generations. If you can cultivate an atmosphere of understanding in your family, you'll find that everyone's communication can improve greatly.

It's difficult to begin to understand people if you don't really listen to what they're saying. Learning how to truly listen to people is the first step toward gaining understanding. Unfortunately, we probably listen to our families the least—we know them so well that when they try to talk to us, we think we already know what they're going to say. We may stop hearing their words, interrupt them, or even try to finish their sentences for them. When we do this, they are completely aware of the fact that we're not listening, and this can cause great frustration. Voices rise, emotions heat up, and pretty soon, the communication breakdown is complete. "You just don't understand!" echoes throughout the room—and of course, it's true. Adults probably have a more difficult time being patient while listening to children, yet it's most important to cultivate an atmosphere of understanding with them. This is how they learn to communicate. If family conversations are thoughtful and unhurried, they will practice speaking this way with others, as well.

Becoming a good listener takes patience and a genuine desire to seek understanding. The next time that you have a conversation with a family member, try this: Pretend that you're listening to a tape or CD that you can't interrupt until it's finished. Really listen, not only to the words being spoken, but to the thoughts and emotions behind the words. When the other person has stopped, don't speak right away. Think about what's been said before giving your response. By making it less of an "emergency" to get your own point across, you'll be able to really take in what was said to you.

Everyone wants to be listened to and understood. When you take the time to do this for others, the people in your life feel special and appreciated because you are willing to understand them. These techniques may not be easy at first, but they're worth practicing for the improvement in family communication and relationships.

67.

Say What You Mean,
and Mean What You Say

This strategy is pretty simple—don't confuse your grandchildren with vague or conflicting messages. Sometimes we say things with our words that don't quite match our actions, leading children to wonder if we are saying what we really mean. Should they trust the things that we say, or should they trust the things that we do?

Suppose the rule in your house is that children are in bed at 10:00. But if they are still up and running around at 10:15 and you don't insist on them going to bed, it seems to them that you don't really mean it when you say that bedtime is 10:00. If you give your grandchildren the impression that you don't mean what you say, they won't take very much of what you say seriously. They will begin to test other limits, and pretty soon, your stress and frustration levels will rise as you wonder why they don't listen to you. You might then raise your voice and become angry, but the children won't understand why you're so upset. After all, you didn't seem to mean what you said about the 10:00 bedtime.

On the other hand, if you really don't mind them being up until 10:30, then don't tell them to be in bed by 10:00. Say what you really mean, and stick with it. It's all about consistency. Be open and honest with your grandchildren when you make rules or give instructions, and be clear about what you want and expect from them. Take time to make sure that they understand. Don't make children guess when you "mean it" and when you don't. You can't expect them to follow rules if you don't enforce them most of the time, and you make it worse if you suddenly become angry and demand that they comply. "This time I really mean it!" simply won't work. By then, you've probably lost them concerning trusting what you say.

Your grandchildren are anxious to please you if they know what you want. By being clear about what you desire from them, you can avoid frustration for everyone and make visits with your grandchildren more peaceful and enjoyable.

68.

Teach Them to Truly
Care About Others

Compassion is a characteristic that seems to be in short supply these days. Yet there are few things in life that are more important to humanity than compassion. One of the greatest gifts that you can give your grandchildren is to help them see life from a different perspective than their own. When they understand and feel sympathy for the lives of others, they learn to feel compassion.

Children can be very focused on themselves and their own needs. However, it can be easy to help them expand their views a bit to include others, because they're so willing to listen and learn from you. Like anything else, developing this expanded view takes some practice. You might start by pointing out the reality of other people's lives. For example, if you see a news story on television about children from a war-torn nation, you might discuss it with your grandchildren by saying, "It's probably hard for you to imagine growing up in a country where there is fighting all the time. What do you think it might be like?" You can talk about how hard life is for these children, how many of them have lost one or both parents, how they might not have enough food or a safe place to stay. Subjects such as this can be difficult, to be sure, and very young children may not be able to grasp some of the concepts. But by showing children that there are people in the world who are living in far worse conditions than they are, you can help them to appreciate what they do have. Then you can guide your grandchildren toward wanting to help in some way. After discussing the plight of children of war, you might search for a charity that helps such children and make a donation together.

Ideally, you want your grandchildren to make compassion and caring for others a part of their lives. Try to find some way to demonstrate this to them every day, even if it's simply saying hello to a stranger you pass on the street. The point is to show your grandchildren that the very act of becoming aware of the lives and situations of others is what really connects us all as human beings.

69.

Pass Along Your
Values by Example

Earlier in this book, we discussed how children are great imitators who love to watch adults, mimic them, and learn from them. You can put this tendency to positive use if you put your values into action for your grandchildren to watch and learn from. Remember that actions speak louder than words, and children can absorb the real lessons without much difficulty. Many kids will tune out talks or lectures, so why not *show* them the positive things that you want them to learn?

There are so many ways to demonstrate values to grandchildren through action. Suppose a harried clerk at the grocery store keeps making mistakes while trying to check out your order. If you smile and show patience and compassion, your grandchildren will see that being kind can be easy, even in the face of a testy situation. You can show your compassion by putting some money into a Salvation Army kettle during the holidays or buying a paper poppy for disabled veterans on Veteran's Day. Explain what the donation is for and why the cause is important. Let your grandchildren place the money into the kettle themselves. Holding a door for someone, helping someone less able, returning extra change given to you in error—there's no end to the possibilities for showing children values just through everyday living.

At the same time, be aware of any negative examples you may be setting. If you're in the car and have a tendency to get upset when you get tied up in traffic, remember that your grandchildren can learn from that kind of behavior, too. In their eyes, you are a role model to be watched and imitated. Knowing this can help you become more aware of your own stressful behaviors and give you pause to take a breath, relax, and be the role model you want to be.

70.

Teach Them About Tradition

Families change and evolve over the years, and too often we can lose precious traditions that make our families unique. Grandchildren can have a strong desire to learn about the family traditions, because it tells them who they are and where they come from. As you seek to bond with your grandchildren, you can help them develop a sense of their own place in the family by teaching them about your traditions and history.

You can begin by bringing back any traditions that you may have lost over the years. A tradition can be anything that the family does together routinely over a period of time, perhaps something passed down across generations. Family reunions, special prayers, or observing holidays in certain fashions are all traditions you may have had. If you remember any rituals from your childhood, why not bring them back for your grandchildren? Think of the good feelings you'll have as you share memories with them.

You can also use your one-on-one talks at bedtime to tell stories about yourself as a child, about your children, and about other family members your grandchildren may know little or nothing about. Imagine their delight as they hear stories about their great-great-grandfather's first car, or the family's country store that was once run by their great-grandmother. Did you have certain holidays or family anniversaries that called for a major gathering every year? Are there photographs, artwork, songs, clothing, or collectibles that have been passed down from generation to generation that tell the unique story of your family? Did you follow religious traditions from generation to generation? All of these things can be important in helping your grandchildren build a sense of belonging to the family. There's nothing that says you can't create new traditions for the family, as well. If you don't usually have family reunions, why not try to organize one and let your grandchildren help you with the details? Some families hold reunions on the birthday of the oldest person in the family. This might be a good place to start.

At the heart of family tradition is love and gratitude for what you have and for those who are a part of your life. Practicing traditions is an opportunity to give thanks together, which brings out the best in everyone. You'll be surprised at how much closer your family can become.

71.

Spend Time Alone
with Your Grandchildren

When you think about your own grandparents, the times you remember best are probably the ones you spent with them alone. The foundation of a grandparent-grandchild relationship can be built by spending time together without the distractions of others.

This isn't always easy. If you don't live in the same town, it may be difficult to get much time alone with your grandchildren when visits do occur. The trip may be short, and there may be many things you want to accomplish. Grabbing little moments here and there may be the best solution. When you're a kid, time seems to stretch on forever. You can probably recall that time started to fly past you faster and faster as you got older. Use your grandchildren's perceptions of time to your advantage. Whatever time you do spend alone together will be savored deeply by the children. That is, after all, what they really want from you—some time and your love.

Even more difficult is finding time alone with individual

children in a sibling group. This is where one-on-one time becomes even more important, so each grandchild can make that special connection and feel equally treated compared to other grandchildren. You don't want anyone to feel left out, but at the same time, it's important for everyone in the family to understand your need for spending time with each individual grandchild alone.

For the long-distance grandparent, time alone can be accomplished by phone, if necessary. Hearing your voice and being able to communicate with you in real time is the next best thing to your being there for your grandkids, particularly if you keep that connection alive regularly.

Just as time can creep by for your grandchildren, it will certainly fly for you. It won't be long before they're grown up. Don't miss the opportunity to make that one-on-one connection with each grandchild.

72.

Practice Participating
by Watching

You look forward to visits with your grandchildren and want to spend time with them. But if you visit them at their home and they are involved with their own friends and activities, don't get upset and demand that they stop what they're doing to spend time with you. Learn to simply take joy in watching them, or jump right in and play along.

You can get so much out of watching young children playing together. Just sit back and observe without speaking to them or interfering, and you'll be reminded of your own childhood. Let your mind wander back to your own youth and some of your favorite play-time activities. Perhaps you'll feel a bit more lighthearted than you did earlier in the day. A smile might replace a frown on your face, or you might burst into hearty laughter. You'll experience a refreshing feeling that can make your troubles seem to disappear.

It's easy to find yourself irritated if you take the time to visit your grandchildren and they are more interested in roughhousing with their friends or being engrossed in a new computer game than in being with you. As they grow and mature, their interests will increase, and it may seem that they have less time for their grandparents. It helps to remember that there is a kind of joy that comes from just being a fly on the wall. Your presence in their home, at their school, or at their games will be remembered much longer than the computer games they play with their friends. If you learn not to take their distractions personally, you can enjoy being a regular and steady presence in their lives—not just someone who demands they drop everything so that they can pay attention to *you*.

73.

Learn to Be Open-Minded
in a Changing World

Your grandchildren live in a world vastly different from the one you remember as a child. They learn and play on computers, and even the youngest of children often carries a pager or cellular phone. Home life to them can often mean single parents or blended families. Your grandson's spiky hair is dyed orange, your teenage granddaughter has a tattoo on her shoulder, and they both speak a slang that you don't understand. Such changes in society and family structures can be perplexing and difficult for many grandparents to accept. All can be sources of conflict and stress within a family. Whatever happened to the "good old days," you wonder?

Being open-minded to the changing world can help restore peace and harmony to your family and reduce the shock factor often present between generations. This doesn't mean that you have to blindly accept new ideas and concepts that conflict with your values. But it's important for you to be open-minded if you are to enjoy time spent with your grandchildren, because the changing world is very much *their* world. By expanding your mind, you can better understand your grandchildren's—and your children's—lives and experiences.

Being open-minded means taking time to learn, examining different points of view, and making a conscious effort to adapt. How can you accomplish these things? You don't have to start speaking the latest slang, wearing the newest fashions, or visiting the local tattoo parlor. But you can read and learn about the origins of these trends and fads. You'll develop a sense of where your grandchildren's generation is coming from, which will help you give them greater understanding along with your love.

The next time your grandchildren change their hair color or get tattoos, don't become upset. Rather, try saying nothing at all and simply accepting it. As you learn to catch the often odd balls this changing world throws at you, you'll discover something remarkable happening—you just might be changing, too. Wouldn't it be nice for your grandchildren to have grandparents who are truly open-minded, not stuffy and set in their ways?

74.

Work to Narrow
the Generation Gap

Just when you thought the generation gap was gone between you and your children—surprise! It opened up again when you became a grandparent. Not only that, but now there's also one of those pesky gaps between your children and *their* children! It seems that the generation gap will always be present in one way or another. Times change, culture and technology move at breakneck speed, and each generation can seem farther away from the other on every topic imaginable. Though at times it may seem impossible, you should be heartened to know that generation gaps *can* be bridged.

The generation gap can really show itself when it comes to child-rearing theories. Amazingly, what was once taken as gospel when you were a new parent may be termed a myth or old wives' tale by experts and physicians today. For example, your doctors probably told you to place your children on their stomachs to sleep in order to prevent accidental choking. Today's prevailing theory is to let children sleep on their backs to prevent Sudden Infant Death Syndrome. Imagine the conflict that this might cause at the child's bedtime between an anxious new parent and a well-meaning grandparent.

It doesn't do any good when one generation tries to push its ideas on another. Bridging the generation gap means keeping an open mind when listening to new ideas and making a commitment to learn more about them. You don't have to agree, but you can at least be informed, understand, and accept that the world is indeed dynamic—changes do happen. Your willingness to learn and understand can open up similar feelings in the younger generations, too, bringing everyone closer together.

75.

Set the Boundaries in Your Home
(but Be Flexible, Too)

Grandchildren need to have rules in your home. Away from their parents, they may feel excitement and a sense of freedom that can entice them to forget about the limits and boundaries that their parents have set for them. Explaining your own set of rules and expectations with a positive attitude will bring them back to reality. In fact, they will be relieved to know that there are guidelines they must follow. Children unconsciously desire and look for boundaries. When they know their limits, they are relieved of the confusion that comes with not understanding what is expected of them.

Conflict may arise if your rules differ from those your grandchildren are used to at home, however. If bedtime in your house is 9:00, but at home it's 10:00, they may resist your rules, saying, "But at home, we're allowed to stay up until ten!" Ideally, you want to have as much consistency as possible between their rules at home and yours. But if yours must be different, the solution to resistance is to stand fast and repeat your rules. "In our house, bedtime is at nine." Don't be afraid to enforce the rules in your own home. You won't lose the love and affection of your grandchildren. But do avoid passing judgement on the rules they have at home. Help them understand that yours are simply different.

You can allow some flexibility in your own mind. This doesn't mean that if grandchildren argue over the rules, you back down and give in to their demands. Rather, you can allow for something special, like taking them to a movie that runs late. In the end, you want your grandchildren to learn to respect your wishes and the sanctity of your home.

76.

Be a Mentor to
Your Grandchildren

Think about a person in your life who really believed in you, inspired you, and gave you the motivation to strive for what you wanted. Was there someone who picked you up when you fell, raised your spirits when you were feeling down, or helped you to go on anytime that you felt like quitting? It may have been a teacher, a close friend, or a family member—possibly a grandparent. Whatever role this person filled in your life, you might also have called this person a mentor. By definition, a mentor is a "friend or sage advisor." What a wonderful role for grandparents to fill for their grandchildren—and they have all the right qualifications to do so.

In fact, a lot of what grandparents do naturally is considered to be mentoring. You're already a coach and a cheerleader for the family. But as a mentor, you can inspire your grandchildren to fulfill their greatest potential and cheer them on as they do. You can also enrich your grandchildren's lives by passing along your knowledge and experiences, lessons learned from a different time and perhaps a different place.

A mentor is a unique combination of teacher, friend, advisor, confidant, "sounding board," ally, and above all, support system. It's not an easy role, but it's one that grandparents can relish and approach with the idea of learning as they go along. Take the role seriously, and know that sometimes you can be a mentor simply by being there for your grandchildren. You'll find that your own life is much more enriched and filled with joy, knowing that you can make a real impact on your grandchildren's lives.

77.

Appreciate
the Whole Family

When your children got married, you didn't just gain a son- or daughter-in-law, you gained that person's family, too. Your grandchildren are blessed with an extended family of aunts, uncles, and cousins from both parents' sides, plus another set of grandparents. For some people, getting along with an extended family can pose unique challenges, because few things call more for the spirit of sharing and compromise. Learning to appreciate your grandchildren's extended family is a challenge worth the effort and understanding it can take to meet.

Today, it is nearly impossible to bring so many people together without finding differences in opinions, values, religion, and even culture. But your children and grandchildren are the common ground, and their best interests are what to work for when striving for extended family relationships that are loving and filled with respect for one another. If others in the extended family have different dining habits, celebrate holidays differently, or even speak a different language, you and your grandchildren can come to appreciate that such diversity is good. The children—and you—can be quite adaptable.

This isn't to say that everything in the whole family—no matter which side—should be accepted or tolerated. Certainly you would want to protect your grandchildren from any dysfunctional aspects that may exist. But it's often the simple, everyday things that can cause ongoing stress and damage to relationships—who gets to see the grandchildren for which holidays, who takes them on vacation, and other unwitting competitions for their attention. How can you avoid all of this? By instilling in yourself, your children, and your grandchildren an appreciation and gratitude for everyone in the family. Focus less on competing with each other and work more toward cooperation—practice acceptance of those who are important in your grandchildren's lives.

If you pass along to your grandchildren an appreciation for people's differences, they can learn a lot about life in a world that's rapidly growing smaller. The important thing is for all of the people in the extended family to love and care about your grandchildren, and that's a point on which everyone should lovingly agree.

78.

Age Is an Attitude

Admit it—when you first became a grandparent, you probably became shockingly aware of your age and the inevitability of aging. Nothing drives home the fact that you're getting older more than when your children start having children of their own. But just because you're now a grandparent doesn't mean that you have to panic or wear a label that says "old and stuffy." Some people can fall into depression, becoming moody or irritable and difficult to be with as they face aging. Now, more than ever, it's important to recognize that age is an attitude, and how you feel about aging is entirely up to you.

Think of aging as a new path ahead of you. You can choose to walk it gracefully, or you can mourn your passing youth. The real secret is to refuse to allow grass to grow under your feet. The fact is that people are living longer, more vital, and healthier lives than ever, and attitude plays a big part in your total well-being. You've probably heard this before, but it's repeated over and over again because it's true: The way to stay young is to think young.

In the past, you made goals and plans and had a lot of things to look forward to. Continuing to set goals and make plans can keep you from feeling that life is passing you by. It's as important now as it was then to make goals and strive to reach them, and the sky can truly be your limit. Was there an exotic trip you always wanted to take, or a skill you wished to acquire? Maybe you wanted to study art, open a small business, or take up a certain hobby. Why not do it now? Keeping yourself active and challenged is one way to walk the path of aging with confidence and ease.

Everywhere you look, you see ads for products that will help you look younger. All the hype is for nothing, however, because you won't find the capacity to age gracefully in any bottle. You will find it right inside yourself and within your own family. Look at your grandchildren and realize that they will help keep you young if you have the right attitude.

In the end, your purpose in aging gracefully is to live your life to the fullest for yourself, your children, and your grandchildren. When you feel good about yourself and about life, the little things won't bother you nearly as much, and your family will enjoy spending time with you. "I'm a grandparent!" is just the beginning of a new phase of life that holds promises of joy and fulfillment for many, many years to come.

79.

Love the Little Things—
There Are So Many

Do you remember your young son's first base hit in Little League? Or the time that your little daughter made you a special birthday breakfast, burnt toast and all? Then there was the time that you all rode a toboggan together, hit a big bump in the middle of the hill, and spilled onto the snow, rolling and laughing all the way. Isn't it amazing how well you recall those moments, as if you had photographs of them? In a way, you do. Much as you treasure the photos of your family vacations, birthdays, graduations, and weddings, there are images of little moments etched into your memory. Those moments— ordinary on the outside but extraordinary on the inside—are the little things you truly love and will never forget.

Each time you are with your grandchildren, appreciate and love the little things like smiles, sunny afternoons, a dab of cake frosting on the nose, or a nursery rhyme sung out of key. These little things enrich and fulfill us. There truly are so many of them to be grateful for. The abundant rewards of grandparenting are found in paying attention to all the tiny moments that can sadly slip away if you don't tune in to them and take advantage of their power to create lasting memories. When your grandchild calls your attention to a drawing she's done, stop and look at it closely, see what she's saying, and then show her how proud you are by hanging the drawing on that great family museum, the refrigerator door. The next time that you're handed a flower, a rock, or a seashell, hear the message— "You're special!"—and treasure that precious gift.

The big moments in your grandchildren's lives will certainly make you proud, and it's fun to anticipate them. But in the end, it's the little things you'll love and treasure the most.

80.

When the Going Gets Tough, Remember That Love Is the Glue

In any family, there are good times and there are not-so-good times. Even the closest of families experiences unavoidable arguments, disagreements, outbursts, or even worse, bad news. It can take a lot of love to help you move past the problems and sad times, and that's when you really want to remember the love that you share for each other. Pulling your thoughts away from what's troubling you and focusing on the special moments you've shared as a family can do wonders to keep you going when the chips are down. Your love can boost your spirits and hold you together.

Family love is something you can count on. Whether things are going badly or everything's coming up roses, your love for your family simply is. It doesn't matter what mood your family members are in or how they behave from one day to the next—you look past these things and give your loved ones the benefit of the doubt. You don't stop loving your grandchild who has had a temper tantrum, nor do you stop loving one of your children who has been short-tempered with you for some reason. To say "I can't love you unless you're always in a good mood" would not only be preposterous; it would place conditions on love. The fact is that unconditional love is the glue that binds you together through bad times.

The next time that you feel stressed because of a conflict or a family problem, take a moment to remember a time when everyone was happy and full of love. It will lift your spirits and help you to see that whatever problem you're facing will pass, and you'll get through it together.

81.

Speak Up When
It Becomes Too Much

One of the greatest sources of tension and resentment in three-generation relationships is when grandparents unwittingly become a baby-sitting service. It often happens unconsciously, and the intentions behind it may be entirely good. But if your children begin to make too much use of your baby-sitting services, speak up before you become overwhelmed.

Of course you love your grandchildren and want to spend as much time as you can with them. You also want to help your children and be supportive of them when they need it. But it's important to keep a clear perspective about how often you're baby-sitting your grandchildren and why, particularly if it begins to interfere with the rest of your life. The motives behind the overabundance of baby-sitting requests can be quite simple: Your children feel far more comfortable leaving their children with you than with a non-family baby-sitter. Calling upon you often is probably done with the children's best interests in mind.

But sometimes guilt—real or imagined—plays a part in these scenarios. Grandparents can feel very guilty saying no to baby-sitting. They want to help their children, so they go ahead and change plans or sacrifice quiet time to take their grandchildren. If grandparents feel put upon and resentful, they can take these feelings out on everyone, including their grandchildren. Then everyone in the family will share the stress and hurt feelings. This is not exactly the kind of sharing you should be striving for.

Another reason a lot of grandparents have difficulty saying no to baby-sitting is that they fear their grandchildren will think they don't want to spend time with them. The truth is that your grandchildren won't notice your refusal unless it turns into a tense situation between you and your children. Whether you have something else to do or simply need your quiet time, reassure your grandchildren that you absolutely love them and want to be with them. If you explain that you simply can't do it, they won't feel rejected.

The best way to avoid conflict is to discuss baby-sitting at family meetings, which are designed for working out just these types of situations. In this safe and healing atmosphere, you can vent any frustrations or feelings of being taken advantage of before they become bigger problems. Working together, you'll likely find solutions to these problems and preserve everyone's feelings all around. The important thing is to speak up and keep the situation from getting out of hand in the first place.

82.

Let Your Grandchildren
Help You

Few things make grandchildren feel more important than being helpful, and kids seem to especially love helping their grandparents. Why not let them pitch in and help you wash and wax the car, do the laundry, rake leaves, or get dinner ready? It's a great way to have fun, quality time together and teach them something valuable about helping others.

Kids may actually pester you to let them help, not only because they want to feel grownup and important, but also because they truly want to please you. It can be easy to brush off their desires to help, especially if the children are very young, but try to look at the situation as a learning and sharing experience.

Letting kids help requires a lot of patience on your part. For one thing, you have to be in the right frame of mind. When grandchildren pitch in, you need to be ready for them to make mistakes and be prepared for the job to take more time to complete than if you did it alone. This is particularly true if the littlest ones are helping. So if you have a task that must be done correctly in a certain time frame, do it yourself. This will save irritation and frustration on your part and hurt feelings for the kids.

Cooking and baking are great activities for kids to lend a hand with. Gardening, cleaning out the garage, and even painting around the house can make use of older children's helping hands, especially if your own hands don't work quite as well as they used to. The great thing about working together with your grandchildren is that simple, mundane chores can go from being "ordinary" to "extraordinary." If you think about it, there's nothing wrong with making a game out of work, and in fact, work can be fun when you do it together. Spending quality time and developing a sense of togetherness are the best results of working with your grandchildren. Above all, the kids feel great about helping you, and the experiences will stay in their memories.

83.

Remember That All Grandchildren
Are Created Equal

If you have more than one grandchild, one of the most difficult issues you can face is favoritism. You probably try very hard to get to know each grandchild personally, to share each one's hopes, dreams, and goals. It's important to remember that each child is truly an individual and to treat them all as such. But at the same time, you want to maintain equality among your grandchildren so that no one feels left out or less loved by you.

Showing favoritism can certainly cause discord in a family. Grandchildren can begin to compete with each other for your attention, setting up rivalries where the end result can only be bad feelings all around. Yet treating all your grandchildren exactly the same can be difficult. You might find yourself drawn toward the smallest grandchild, the one who gets sick more than the others, or the shy one who needs extra help meeting and talking to others. Conversely, the ones who excel in school and shine in public may pull you closer with their personal magnetism, a situation that can truly damage the self-esteem of other grandchildren.

It's true that some kids will have special needs, perhaps requiring more attention than the rest. The trick is to be able to provide what's needed while keeping a level playing field for all your grandchildren so that no one feels ignored or overlooked. You need to make them all feel equally loved. Make an extra effort to apply the same rules to all grandchildren, to avoid taking sides in their squabbles with each other, and to lavish equal praise on all. Sometimes you may need to think in reverse—rather than be upset with the child who's less well-behaved, try lavishing even more attention on him. It could be that his misbehavior comes from seeking more attention from you in the first place, and providing that for him may change his behavior. And while you're thinking about equality, be sure to give your adult children a hug for every one you give your grandchildren. You don't want them to feel left out, so remind them how much they are loved and cherished, too.

There's no one easy way to avoid showing favoritism, except to be continuously aware of the possibility and make an extra effort to spread your love around evenly. At the heart of the issue of favoritism is the broader message of sharing. By sharing your love and attention as equally as you possibly can, you create a spirit of sharing and togetherness in all of your grandchildren, and bring the whole family even closer together.

84.

Agree to Agree (or Disagree) About
Discipline and Other Matters

You and your children won't agree about everything regarding your grandchildren and how they're being raised. Does that surprise you? You might think that because you raised your children in a certain way, they will also raise their children in the same way. The fact is that times change, people change, theories and practices of child-rearing and discipline change, and your children may very well see things much differently than you do.

We all have a tendency to want to make others see things our way. This can lead to great frustration and annoyance when they don't. But the world—or your family life—won't suddenly become perfect if you can just turn your children around to your way of thinking. So whenever you and your children disagree about some aspect of how your grandchildren are being raised, remember that trying to change each other's opinions won't get you anywhere.

The best way to head off all of that frustration in the first place is to accept that you won't change each other's minds. Instead of becoming upset when your points of view don't match, see if you can actually appreciate your children's independence and the fact that they see things differently. Rather than react to your differences, talk about them and agree up front to agree—or disagree—about the various aspects of how your grandchildren are being raised. At the same time, pledge your support to their efforts and ask their support for yours, bearing in mind that you are all working for a common goal: the well-being of your grandchildren.

This is not necessarily a topic for hashing out in family team meetings. It is best handled in private between you and your children, without involving your grandchildren. Talk about forms of discipline, rules, boundaries at your home and theirs, and any other subjects involving your grandchildren that could potentially cause conflict and stress in the family. When you do, always keep in mind that just because your children may hold different views or opinions on child-rearing than you do, it doesn't mean that their ways are wrong and yours are right. It simply means that you both have your own views.

If you use this strategy of acceptance and know that you don't necessarily have to agree with each other's ways of thinking, you can keep communication channels open, and thus compromise on matters that might become sticky points. You'll find that this change in attitude can serve to strengthen your family bond.

85.

Express Your Feelings

When you're feeling a little low, you probably want to be graceful about it. You might want to be alone to contemplate a problem or let a bad mood pass so as not to let it interfere with others in your family. However, your grandchildren might not understand what's going on if you suddenly isolate yourself from them without any explanation. This can hurt their feelings, adding to an already existing low mood.

That's why it's important for you to express your feelings. Your grandchildren will learn to understand that at times, everyone feels badly. It's okay for your grandchildren to see you feeling sad or even crying. You probably try to keep your chin up all of the time for them, knowing that they look to you for strength and comfort. Or perhaps you have difficulty expressing feelings, positive or negative, because you may believe that doing so is a sign of weakness. But expressing your feelings and letting your family know when you're upset or feeling badly about something won't change how they feel about you at all. In fact, if you open up and let them know how you're feeling, you're opening yourself to receiving their love, sympathy, and comfort. You want to always be there to help and comfort your family, but they want to be there to help you whenever you might need it, too. The truth is that there is great strength in being comfortable enough with your emotions to express them to others and let them in to help you.

In some ways, this strategy is saying to "lighten up," but with a different meaning than you might think. Sometimes the source of frustration and anxiety is the feelings we carry around inside us. If we can express our feelings and lighten the load we carry, we can release a lot of stress and whittle the small stuff back down to size where we can handle it.

86.

Give Them Space—
Near You and Away from You

Everyone needs some private space, a place where you can be alone to attend to your spiritual needs in whatever manner you choose, sit quietly without distractions, or just read, think, or listen to music in peace, away from the rest of the family. Children are no different. They like to have private spaces, too. They like the security of having a place that's meant to be theirs. When your grandchildren come to visit, they certainly want to be with you, but just as you need private space, make sure to provide them with a place at your home that's all their own.

If you had to share a bedroom when you were a child, remember how badly you wanted to have a room of your own? To you, that was a sign of growing up. Private space not only makes kids feel more grownup and important, it helps them feel good about themselves. You might designate a guestroom as a child's private space when she visits. Make it hers by providing a toy box or trunk to store toys and any other favorite items she may have brought from home. If she didn't bring much with her, you might get certain items—blankets, stuffed toys, pillows—that are exclusively hers and can be her "favorites" whenever she's visiting you. You can also make temporary "private space" if you don't have a lot of room in your home. Clear out a corner of the garage or basement and make it like a "secret clubhouse" for the child. Or perhaps build a tree house together, pitch a tent in the backyard, or make a blanket tent in a corner of the den. Your granddaughter will appreciate whatever effort you put into finding some private space for her. Next, explain where your private space is, and teach your granddaughter to respect your privacy and property at the same time that you respect her private space.

Just remember that your grandchildren do want to be near you, so give them their own space that's close to you, too. If you spend a lot of time in the family room, for example, give them their own small "nook" in the room, perhaps with a desk or table and chairs so that they can draw, color, play games, or read books while they "hang out" with the rest of the family. Make it a space that to them is as familiar and comfortable as your favorite chair is to you. It's another way to let them know that they belong in the family and in your life, and that's the most comfortable feeling they can have.

87.

Be a Storyteller

Do you have fond memories of bedtime stories? Unfortunately, a lot of kids today go to bed with the television or stereo ringing in their ears. The tradition of telling bedtime stories is a ritual that all of our children could do well by. Who better to keep such a great bonding activity alive than grandparents?

The truth is that you don't have to limit being a storyteller to bedtime. Pick any time your grandchildren are receptive to regale them with wonderful tales of your own life and the family history. You can always read to them from books, but why not make up some stories of your own, filled with positive messages about the things you want to teach your grandchildren? Not all stories have to be instructive or educational, of course. Let yourself go, and just be creative making up stories that fascinate and entertain. Encourage your grandkids to tell you stories, too. The important thing is sharing.

There is one slight drawback to being a storyteller: You do have to come up with new material. Most people can probably remember someone in the family who told the same story over and over while everyone else rolled their eyes and said, "Oh, no, not again!" Be sure to stay fresh, and the kids will come back for more.

Everyone needs a break from reality, and getting wrapped up in a well-told story is a great way for kids to do that—and for you, too. Anytime that you all sit down together to tell stories is precious time spent with each other and a simple pleasure in life that can bring joy and closeness. It's said that the best things in life are free, and this certainly qualifies. Give story time a try, and you'll be pleased with the results.

88.

Value Your Own Wisdom

Grandparents can try so hard not to interfere with their children's parenting that they can actually overdo it. If that happens, you are failing to fulfill one of the most important roles of grandparenting. Don't sell yourself short—you have wisdom and knowledge to impart to your family. It can be a tricky thing, however, when you know you have advice that could help your children or grandchildren, but they show little interest in hearing from you. Here's a strategy that will make the advice easier for them swallow.

Your grandchildren probably love to listen to your stories about what things were like when you were their age growing up. It helps them make a special connection to you when they realize that you really *do* know what it's like to be their age. The trick is to not simply tell a story, but to convey the wisdom gained from it. Ask yourself the questions: What did you learn from the experience? Why is this important for your grandchildren to know? What can they learn about you—and about themselves—from this story? Your

197

grandchildren may know you as someone who has always had a love of education and learning. But did they know that as a child, you loved school so much that you would go to any length to get there? The very idea that someone could like school that much could come as quite a shock to some young ones, and perhaps cause them to rethink their own feelings about school. This is the value of your wisdom, so don't be afraid or embarrassed to share your stories that have much to teach.

Your wisdom is worth not only the value you put on it, but what it means to your family, too. It's said that experience is the best teacher, and you've learned a lot. Open up, share your wisdom with your family, and let your experiences enrich everyone's lives. If you are clever, they may never know that they are getting a piece of advice along with that memorable tale.

89.

Realize Your Significance and Take Your Role Seriously

Grandparents sometimes don't realize how important their role is in their grandchildren's lives. Those who live some distance away from their grandchildren are even more likely to downplay their role. But being clear about your role as an integral part of the family is essential to forging a meaningful relationship with your grandchildren.

As a grandparent, you are like a magnet that draws the family to its center. By simply being there, you can provide a feeling of security in a changing world. The family looks to you for guidance, and often your children and grandchildren will follow your lead as to the tone and climate of the family's life. If you are peaceful and relaxed, taking each day as it comes and moving with the flow rather than reacting to what happens, your family will learn to live this way, as well. Reflect on this whenever you find yourself becoming irritated by troubles that you know will pass sooner or later.

It is a lucky child who has grandparents. Just ask the family that isn't fortunate enough to have grandparents still with them. What greater gift can you give children than the love of another human being who is so intimately connected to them?

Often your influence is subtle, and you may not realize its impact or strength until much later, when a surprise incident or comment from a grandchild reveals it. Maybe it's in the way he has learned a certain value or belief from you—being kind to animals, tending to plants correctly, or displaying excellent manners. Whenever grandchildren do this, you realize that they have learned from you and that you have woven yourself into the very fabric of their lives.

Take the step now, and acknowledge that you are indeed very important to them. Know that being out of sight does not mean that you are out of their thoughts and hearts. Keeping that in mind will help you live each day to the fullest, knowing that every moment spent with your family in person or through your lasting influence is precious.

90.

Take Care of Yourself

There are many reasons to make a special effort to take care of yourself. You are the very best reason, of course. Your children and grandchildren are the other two best reasons. There's truth in the old saying, "Healthy body, healthy mind," and being healthy in both areas can help you face life with less stress and more clarity.

If you think back to the last time you were down with a cold or the flu, you'll probably remember how badly you wanted to get over it. Your schedule was off, you felt depressed, and you were miserable to those around you. You could have avoided a lot of stress if you hadn't been ill. It's unrealistic to think that even with good care, you'll never get sick again, but paying more attention to your health can certainly lessen the severity and frequency of illness when it does strike.

Everyone can take a closer look at their health habits and find some room for improvement. Start with your diet—is it time to give up some fried foods, drink more water during the day, or consider taking some supplements? How are you doing with exercise? If you're not active enough, your grandchildren can certainly get you going. Ride bikes, jump rope, or just take walks together to increase your level of activity. You might also introduce the kids to gardening or do other chores around the house together like painting. All of these things count as physical exercise, and they are a lot more fun when you do them with your grandkids. Be sure you get enough sleep each night—which you can always supplement with naps, if needed. And don't forget mental exercise to challenge your mind and keep it sharp. Play word games with the kids, do crossword puzzles, and read and study current events.

Taking care of yourself means your spiritual self, as well as your physical and mental selves. Setting aside time each day for whatever soothes your soul and gives you inner peace is as important as eating right and exercising. Sit quietly alone, meditate, write poetry, do yoga, read, or pray—just be sure to do it regularly. Remember that the best reason for taking care of yourself is you, and your family will be glad that you did.

91.

Make Music Together

This may seem like an unusual suggestion, but the truth is that music has charms that can bring people together, soothe the soul, and lift the spirits. Just try to be negative or depressed while belting out an upbeat, happy song. It's pretty difficult, especially if you sing something like "Happy Days Are Here Again." Music is an excellent way for you to chase away your grandchildren's blues.

Every now and then, sing just for the sake of doing it, even if you do it alone. Making music can bring you joy and serenity. It's no wonder that the spiritual rituals of many different beliefs generally include some type of music. Let your grandchildren hear you singing. Singing along to the radio in the car, humming while you're walking, or making up silly songs together can encourage them to make music part of their daily lives. You don't have to have specific musical talents to make beautiful music together. Anyone can sing "Row, Row, Row Your Boat" if they know the words and the tune. You can even have fun banging the rhythms on pots and pans if it doesn't bother your neighbors.

Perhaps a member of your family plays an instrument. If so, you may be able to spark your grandchildren's interest in studying music and learning to play. But it really doesn't matter. The act of making music together can draw people closer and make the problems and tribulations of everyday life seems a lot less significant. Remember, music can make you lighthearted, and anytime you can laugh, you can make others around you feel much better, too.

92.

Be a Cheerleader

Earlier in this book, you read about the family team and how grandparents can function as coaches of the team. But grandparents wear several hats, and one they should try on often is that of cheerleader.

As cheerleader for your grandchildren, you're there to encourage them as they learn and grow. When they get good grades in school, for example, praise them and let them know how proud you are. If they need to work a bit harder, you're behind them all the way, helping guide them whenever you can and letting them know how much you love them. Your children need cheerleaders, too, so let them know what a terrific job they're doing raising your grandchildren. And be sure to liberally use the most important cheer of all: "I love you."

Some people can go through their entire lives without hearing many words of support or encouragement from those that they love. It's quite sad, and yet it's so easy to remedy. Being a cheerleader to point out your loved one's positive attributes is the perfect balance to people's natural tendency toward negative thinking and focusing on imperfections. Amazingly, most people find it far easier to think negatively and zero in on their mistakes and missteps than they do to talk to themselves positively and give themselves credit for what they've done right.

Everyone wants to be told that they're okay, that others appreciate them and what they're doing, and that things will work out when the chips are down. Your family will be grateful to receive your encouragement and support, so be free with it. After all, there's no greater gift in return than their smiles and their love.

93.

Ask for Your
Grandchildren's Opinions

This idea is especially important when you are grandparenting older children who are forming independent ideas and opinions and can't wait to spread them around. Who better to share those opinions with than loving, understanding grandparents? But for all of your grandchildren, young and old, asking for their opinions and listening with the idea of understanding them helps you get to know who the children are becoming. Everyone has a need to be heard and understood by the people they love, and this is equally true of children.

You don't have to ask the grandkids' opinions on the state of the world financial crisis unless, of course, you have a grandchild who is an international banker. Seeking opinions regarding the little, everyday things in life can make a grandchild feel extra special. Imagine how terrific a child might feel if her grandma said to her, "I'm planning a trip with Grandpa. Do you have any ideas about where I should go?" Or how a young boy would feel whose grandfather said to him, "I know you read a lot of car magazines, and I'm thinking about buying this new model that everyone's talking about—what do you think about that?" You may find that your grandchildren's opinions are more important to you than you might have previously thought. As you listen to what they have to say, look for your own influence in their words. Remember, they do look to you as a role model, so don't be surprised to find that they hold a lot of the same opinions that you do. On the other hand, they may have completely different opinions, and that's okay, too. Your grandchildren are individuals, and you want to show them that what they think and feel counts. You will love them no matter what their opinions are.

94.

Roll with the Punches

There are some things that you can control in life, and many more things that you can't. One of the biggest sources of irritation, conflict, and struggle is our tendency to insist that life must go along exactly as we have planned. The fact is that life is dynamic. It changes from moment to moment. And as soon as children or grandchildren enter the mix, all bets are off. If you want to enjoy life and live with serenity and peace of mind, then you must learn to roll with the punches.

When the best-laid family plans fall through, or ideas and activities go awry, or the mess in the house gets bigger than ever, just roll with it. Stand knee-deep in the flow of life and move with it, not against it. Consider that if you don't go with the flow, you just might miss something along the way. Not accepting what is may blind you to what you might discover. Often things happen for a reason, and perhaps we shouldn't question those reasons too much. There can be a wonderful synchronicity at work in change, and we should be open to go wherever it leads us.

Life with grandchildren will certainly bring a lot of change and plenty of life's little punches your way from time to time. You can live with less stress and more peace if you begin to work with what is and help everyone in the family learn to develop this skill of adapting to whatever might come your way. If you are mentally and emotionally flexible, you can roll with the punches, flowing with and within the flow of life with beauty, style, and grace.

95.

Expect to Make Mistakes

You want to be the perfect grandparent, but alas—you can't be. Most of the things you do will be right on, but the simple fact is that you will make mistakes, and so will the people that you love. It's part of being human.

Many people get hung up on mistakes that they've made, refusing to learn from them or let go of them. They agonize over what was done, get angry at themselves and possibly others, and put themselves through a lot of misery. Even worse, if they don't learn from their mistakes, they are likely to repeat them and end up going through the same misery again and again.

As a grandparent, you should expect to make mistakes—with the grandkids, with your children, with the in-laws. Sometimes you'll say the wrong thing. You might offer advice at a time when you know you should really step aside and keep quiet. You might overstep your children's authority as parents, break one of their rules, show a little favoritism to one grandchild over another, or inadvertently upset one of your in-laws. These things can happen, and they're not the end of the world. In fact, the mistakes mentioned all have the potential to be fixed with little or no harm done.

The important thing about making mistakes is to remember them and therefore keep from repeating them. Mistakes are great teachers, and if you take the time to learn from them, you're far less likely to make the same ones again. But in order to learn from life's little errors, you first have to admit that you make them. This can be extremely difficult for people who feel that they have to do everything perfectly. Everyone makes mistakes, and nobody is perfect. These are two old, often-repeated adages, to be sure, but so important to accept. Take the pressure off of yourself to always be perfect.

If you expect to make mistakes, you won't react impulsively when you do make them. Your mind will be more willing to accept what has happened and begin right away to look for the lesson learned so you won't repeat the mistake. The best way to start changing your attitude is to look at past mistakes and the consequences. You'll probably see that the mistakes really weren't such a big deal, and that things generally worked out okay in the end. Reinforce that thought by remembering a few instances where you didn't make mistakes, and you're on your way to being more accepting of—and less stressed out by—the ones that you do make.

96.

Listen to Your Children and
Respect Their Rights

One of the most important things you can do to prevent conflict and stress in your family life is to listen to your adult children and respect them as parents. Though you've raised your own children and have a lot of experience, you're no longer in charge. It's now your children's turn to be parents, and most likely, they have their hands full. Naturally, you want to help them as much as possible by giving them advice, but what your children need most right now is your ear. They need you to be supportive and to listen to them. It can be a challenge to balance the important role you play in your grandchildren's development with your responsibility to take a passive stance with your own children.

Unsolicited advice, criticism, and judgement can greatly strain the relationship with your children. Your grandchildren will certainly know if there is tension surrounding the adults, too. As parents, your children have a right to raise their own children in their own way. They need to make their own mistakes and set their own rules while you offer support and encouragement. If your children are new at parenting, they are probably filled with insecurities—the same ones you probably felt with your firstborn. In this case, it really helps to remember what it was like when your parents first became grandparents. Sure, you may have stumbled along and made mistakes, but with the love, caring, and support of your own parents, you found your own way.

Listening to your children not only shows that you respect them as parents, but it's your guide to what actions you can and should take. You might make a suggestion or two, but make sure you give them choices and options. This way, they will feel as if they still have control of their own situation.

What if your kids choose to do something you disagree with? Learn to accept their choices, no matter how the situation turns out. Judging their decisions after the fact won't help, and may only be self-serving.

It can be difficult to zip your lip and let your children live their own lives, but always remember to keep your ears open and a shoulder clear for them to lean on. That's what they need from you the most.

97.

Ground Your
Teenage Grandchildren

You probably remember your children's teenage years well—how on earth could you forget? There were times of great happiness and joy, of course, but teen years are better known for the drama and rebellion of children becoming adults.

These can be emotionally charged years. Along with choosing colleges, deciding on career directions, attending proms and making new friends, adolescence brings a change in focus for kids. They tend to turn inward, away from their families. They may see parents less as authority figures and more as "guardians" who are constantly making rules without understanding a single thing about them or their lives! Such drama can be commonplace in teenage years, making it tough for parents and grandparents to deal with the insecure, confused new person that's emerging. Grandparents have an opportunity to really shine during this time. They can fill an important role in the family by grounding their teenage grandchildren.

This doesn't mean punishing them, but rather grounding them in reality by acting as a buffer in the emotional turmoil that so often swirls between teens and their parents. Think of yourself as neutral territory. You aren't—or at least shouldn't be—actively engaged in this "battle." At a time when teens begin to pull away from their parents, it can be natural, almost instinctual, for them to drift toward the neutral ground of their grandparents for support and comfort when the "war" heats up. Grandma and Grandpa represent safety and security, something that isn't lost on their worried parents, either. It's a connection to the family at a time when they feel almost compelled to cut some connections. If the kids run to you when the chips are down, it's better than the possible alternatives.

How do you ground them? Work toward tolerance and understanding of what they're going through by learning about their lifestyles, not criticizing them. Let the teens talk, and just listen. When they want you to talk to them, you'll know it—teenagers usually want what they want on their own terms. Pass along your wisdom, experiences, and values when they're ready to receive them. Let them know that you'll provide them with a compassionate, stress-free environment. Sometimes the best connections between grandparents and teenagers are made during moments of quiet, simple pleasure such as while fishing, driving somewhere, or sharing a bowl of popcorn. And if the grandkids are with you, their parents will have some much-needed "down time" to cool off, too.

Teenage grandchildren can sometimes make you feel tired, but if you jump into your nurturing role with energy and vigor, they'll end up keeping you young and healthy. You're the family team coach and cheerleader, remember? You're also the lightning rod that grounds and insulates everyone from the storm. Be proud of that role, and embrace it.

98.

Remember What You
Learned from Being a Parent

One of the best strategies you can turn to anytime you might find yourself at a loss in dealing with your grandchildren is to ask yourself what you can draw from your experiences as a parent. While grandparenting is a different role with different responsibilities, it can still be a chance to use lessons learned from parenting, and there are probably plenty—both overt and subtle. The benefit comes from remembering what worked for you, and also what didn't work.

Do you ever say to yourself, "I wish I had done this differently"? While you shouldn't be trying to relive your past, nor anguish over past mistakes, you can certainly look at them as learning experiences and use what you've learned to improve your relationships with your children and grandchildren. Maybe you wish that you had encouraged your daughter's artistic leanings more than you did. Today, as an adult, you see her seeking a creative outlet by taking painting lessons, and it bothers you to realize that she could have done that as a child. Rather than be upset with yourself for what is done, help encourage your grandchildren's talents, wherever they may lie. So if you discouraged your daughter from applying to art school, applaud your granddaughter when she tells you that she's taking a photography course. Your support and approval will boost her self-esteem and create a warm bond between you.

Likewise, you may recall being a bit too hard on your son for one thing or another. Maybe you just feel that you didn't hug him as much as you should have. You can try to talk with him about it now, share your feelings, and discuss any revelations you may have had regarding that issue. In doing so, you might suggest that you could both learn from what happened. Maybe your grandson will benefit from this. Both of you can make a special effort to give as many hugs as possible, and that can make everyone feel good.

It does no one in the family any good when you beat yourself up for things that you feel you could have or should have done differently. Admitting that you have made mistakes can take the pressure off. Helping your children to keep from making the same mistakes with their children is not only a way to mend things in your own mind; it reduces a lot of stress and makes life better for you, your children, and your grandchildren.

99.

"Forgive and Forget"
Is More Important Than Ever

In the three-generation family, there are many intricate relationships at work, many feelings and egos, and a lot of potential for hurt and carrying grudges. The concept of "forgive and forget" is truly more important than ever.

To forgive is to let go of anger and resentment. It's easy to point to a reason for being angry with someone and retain that anger. But does that issue hold up? Look for a more compelling reason to let go of your anger. Where your family is concerned, this should be easy. Say you're angry at your grandchild for breaking a vase. In this example, finding the reason to let go of your anger is simple: A broken object, no matter how expensive or sentimental it might be, isn't a good enough reason to carry a grudge or hang on to angry feelings toward your grandchild. On the other hand, your family's happiness and peace, and having a good relationship with your grandchild, are very compelling reasons to let go of the anger.

When you look at it this way, you can easily see what's more important in your life. You accept and understand that no one is perfect, including yourself, and that makes you realize that you would want to be forgiven, as well.

To forget can be just as easy. Simply ask yourself how much the situation will mean a year from now. Whether it's a broken vase, an emotional outburst, a special date forgotten, or a canceled visit, you probably won't give it a thought a year from now. If you keep that in mind, the problem will quickly disappear, and you can get back to the business of enjoying life with your family.

Be mindful that tomorrow is another day. The little things are likely to look very different and less significant than they do today. "Forgive and forget" is *not* a cliché—it's a phrase to truly live by to be a happier, more peaceful, and content person.

100.

Remember That They Will Always Remember You

Throughout this book, you have been encouraged to remember your own grandparents, to look back to your own experiences as a grandchild, and to draw on those memories to help you become a terrific grandparent yourself. You probably did that unconsciously anyway. Your grandparents may not have given a single thought to the possibility that their great-great-grandchildren would feel any influence from them, and they probably didn't consider that grandparenting means being a role model.

Your grandchildren will always remember you as they become parents and eventually grandparents themselves. You are the model of grandparenting that they will look upon and refer to when they want to remember "how it was done." They will have imprinted on their memories the wonderful legacy you will leave them, a legacy of being together that they can pass along to future generations. Their memories will include images of you as a source of wisdom and experience, as the anchor of the family, and as someone who shared with love, caring, and respect for all. Your ideals will be passed along, through words and by example—family is important and to be treasured, and time together is precious.

Start today to build that legacy. Make each visit with your grandchildren really count, and make family time together special. Fill your lives—and your children's and grandchildren's—with love, appreciation, and gratitude. And most of all, practice each day so that you don't sweat the small stuff, and so that you enjoy this wonderful life to its fullest.